The Complete Guide
to Raised Bed
Gardening

The Complete Guide
to Raised Bed
Gardening

Maximize Your Harvest with Less Effort!

Grow Your Own Vegetables, Fruits, and Herbs
with Sustainable, Budget-friendly DIY Solutions
and Gardening Techniques

Written by Sophie McKay
www.SophieMcKay.com

First edition, 2024

ISBN 978-1-916662-29-2 (paperback)
ISBN 978-1-916662-30-8 (ebook)
ISBN 978-1-916662-31-5 (hardback)

Website: www.SophieMcKay.com
Email: Sophie@sophiemckay.com
Author page: https://www.facebook.com/Sophie.McKay.Author
Facebook: www.facebook.com/groups/garden.to.table.tribe

Table of content

Looking for a gardening companion?

This Garden Planner is the perfect choice.

This guide is your trusty companion for planning, tracking, and celebrating the life in your garden, ensuring you enjoy every step of your gardening journey. Inside this logbook, you'll discover:

- **Dream Garden Planner**: Define your ideal garden and make it a reality.
- **Comprehensive Inventories**: Keep track of your **tools, seeds, roots, bulbs, shopping lists, and expenses**.
- **Seasonal Chore Planners**: Stay on top of your gardening tasks in every season, from early spring through to winter.
- **Garden Layout and Sun Map**: Plan your garden strategically.

- **Planting Timelines and Health Tracking**: Get insights on when to sow and harvest while **keeping an eye on rainfall, pests, and diseases**.
- **Pollinator Fan Page**: Celebrate the vibrant and your garden's ecosystem.
- **Tips&Tricks:** Dive deeper into gardening with **Square-Foot Gardening basics, a Companion Planting guide, the grow-bag cheat sheet** and more.

Just scan this QR code with your phone or visit the https://Gardenplanner.SophieMckay.com link to land directly on the book's Amazon page.

Introduction

My gardening journey started in the backyard of my small home many years ago. My first few attempts at growing vegetables were anything but promising. But a few years down the road, I managed to transform my dismal garden patch into a cornucopia of leafy greens and juicy fruits. The secret? Raised beds.

Introducing a raised bed in my backyard marked a turning point. My garden started to flourish! I could grow a wide variety of plants in my limited space and enjoy a bountiful harvest. Moreover, I no longer had to worry about rabbits and my neighbor's cat ruining my garden patch.

When I think about my early days as a gardener, I can't help but admit that it wasn't always smooth sailing. However, with the help of sustainable gardening practices, I eventually maximized my returns and carved my own success.

I was new in town, with little experience. Even though I'd grown up at my grandparents' farm, tending to my own vegetable patch and fruit trees was new territory. Naturally, I made mistakes. Lots of them! It wasn't long before I realized I needed to learn more about my surroundings.

One morning, an idea struck me as I stared out the window. I hurried into my backyard, plucked the few pale, shriveled lettuce leaves and stunted tomatoes I'd managed to grow, and placed them in a basket. Putting on my hat, I hooked it on my arm, the disappointing harvest on full display, and set off to meet my neighbors.

My shortcomings aside, at least I was confident. The bewildered look on my neighbors' faces, when I presented them with a few wilting greens, tasteless berries, and flavorless tomatoes, makes me smile to this day. With the introductions out of the way, we formed a camaraderie, bonding over our love for growing our own crops.

My kind neighbors would drop by my house and we'd swap seeds and plants over steaming cups of coffee. Their knowledge of the local climate, soil, and native plants proved invaluable. I quickly learned that the soil in my backyard lacked the qualities required to grow healthy plants. But instead of feeling discouraged, I set out to find a solution.

The quest to have my own kitchen garden introduced me to the idea of raised beds. I'll admit, I was intimidated at first. It was clear to me that if I wanted my plants to thrive, I had to push through. So I added raised beds to my garden, tended to my plants while keeping various environmental factors in mind, made decisions based on fluctuating weather patterns, and anticipated possible mishaps. And, soon, I had an impressive harvest to show for my hard work.

There was only one problem now: I had more produce than I could handle. Wasting it wasn't an option, so the excess went into pickle jars, cans, or dips (pesto, tomato sauce, chutney, you name it!). Eventually, I produced enough to sell at the local market. My sauces were a hit! The delicious fruits and vegetables from my garden quickly became town favorites!

The profits rolling in helped me scale up. Gradually, I shifted to renewable energy, decreased my expenses by using sustainable systems, and started using my resources more efficiently. Over the years, I've had tremendous success as a grower and a teacher. I've taught sustainable gardening methods to hundreds of people the world over. My interactions with other gardening enthusiasts around the globe left me feeling humbled and inspired.

After all these years, I'm grateful I didn't let the failures I encountered at the beginning of my journey discourage me from trying again. I'm glad I persevered or I would never have experienced the things I did.

Looking back, I'm amazed how all this can be traced back to that one raised bed I clumsily constructed from scavenged wood in my backyard.

So what are raised beds and why do growers love them?

Well, the idea is certainly nothing new, farmers have been doing it for centuries. Growing plants in mounded soil has been around for quite some time. What makes raised-bed gardening unique is the significantly higher soil level compared to the ground around it. Ranging from 6 inches to waist-high, the sturdy frames of raised beds prevent soil spillage and maximize space. The design allows growers to build 3 to 4 feet wide planting beds.

While it may appear daunting at first sight, growing fruits and vegetables in raised beds requires little experience. Whether you're a beginner or a skilled grower, sustainable gardening is well within your reach. I've compiled in this book all the techniques required to create a long-term, sustainable garden. From selecting raw materials to clever planting and watering techniques to maximize your yield, you'll find it all.

This book will provide you with an easy step-by-step guide for building your own raised garden bed. I'm a firm believer in not being discouraged by space constraints and this book will show you how to utilize what you have and turn it into an asset. You don't need acres of land to meet your food needs. All that's required is a little dedication and lots of passion to nurture and watch your plants grow.

Once you're off to a solid start, you don't have to worry about what comes next because *Raised-Bed Gardening* has you covered. Here, you'll find a plethora of information about planting, selecting plant varieties, growing, and harvesting. By the time you finish reading, you'll have a good grip on the ins and outs of raised-bed gardening, the materials required, and the challenges you may encounter.

We're starting things off by discussing the multitude of benefits of raised-bed gardening in Chapter 1 followed by planning your garden layout in Chapter 2. In Chapters 3 and 4, we'll look at how to build raised beds and assess soil health. Chapter 5 is all about plant prep before you sow the first seed.

Chapters 6 and 7 will cover planting guidelines, growing requirements, and harvesting techniques. Chapter 8 marks the end of the book by shedding light on some common problems associated with raised-bed gardening and ways to solve them.

As a gardening enthusiast with over ten years of experience, I don't think there's anything as rewarding as growing your own food. Whether soaring food prices have got you in a fix or you simply want to cut out unwanted chemicals from the food you eat, a sustainable home garden is just what you need. With *Raised-Bed Gardening*, you'll find the confidence required to take the first big step and plant the seed.

So let go of your doubts and embark on this exciting journey with me. Let's explore the fascinating world of raised-bed gardening, and how it could help you unlock your gardening potential.

Chapter 1

Why Do We Love Raised-Bed Gardening?

Plants are finicky creatures. Without the right conditions, they refuse to thrive. They'll show their displeasure with their environment in numerous ways. Yellowing leaves, stunted growth, scarce harvest, and flavorless fruits. If they're unhappy, you can count on them to let you know!

This is when a raised bed comes in handy. In areas with hard, infertile soil, raised beds can help plants flourish. Growing plants in a contained environment allows growers more control over the soil, improving the plant's survival and leading to more produce. Confined to a smaller area, the soil retains moisture longer, limiting water waste. This way, you can create the perfect conditions for your plants, no matter where you live!

Let's take a closer look at raised beds and everything they have to offer.

A Beginner's Guide to Raised Beds

A raised bed can be anywhere from a few inches tall to waist-high and made with different materials. Generally, there's enough space on the outside for you to walk around, which minimizes soil compaction.

Loose, fluffy soil is a must for plant roots to give them plenty of room to breath and absorb water.

While a frame is an important design feature, the choice of material varies based on personal preferences. Traditionally, the frames are constructed with wood or sturdy plastic. However, you can also use a wide range of other materials such as stones, patio pavers, cinder blocks, broken concrete pieces bricks, corrugated metal, and even straw bales! Keeping your personal style and landscape in mind, you can customize it to your liking.

Regardless of what it's made of, a raised bed is ideally narrow enough for you to reach the center from either side. While its length may vary, the width should not be more than 4 feet.

Depth can also be variable, depending on what you choose to grow. For instance, deep-rooted plants such as mini fruit trees or tomatoes require more soil in comparison to shallow-rooted plants like pansies or lettuce. If you suffer from back problems, you can elevate the beds on your legs to avoid stooping.

The base of the bed isn't necessary, though it may be helpful to have one. A fine mesh hardware cloth can keep out gophers and other critters, protecting your plants. A solid base with good drainage is also an excellent option for decks and patios.

Perhaps the best feature of raised beds is the ability to modify soil. This ensures gardening success, especially in areas where the soil is rich in clay and drains poorly. Newly constructed areas are more prone to these problems due to soil compaction. With better control of your plants' soil, you can amend it according to your plants' needs, fulfilling their nutritional requirements with ease.

Lawns, patios, rooftops, or even concrete—you can build raised beds almost anywhere you like. The sky's the limit! This makes it perfect for urban gardening. Gardening enthusiasts living in small spaces no longer have to put their passion on the backburner. Raised beds offer practical and versatile solutions to a number of problems, making them a must for growing healthy plants, maximizing space, and gardening with convenience.

Where do I start? There are countless reasons to love them! From the ability to grow a wide range of plants to gardening with ease, raised beds are known for the numerous advantages they have to offer.

Soil in raised beds warms and drains more quickly during spring, extending the growing season. This may give gardeners a few more weeks to grow crops of their choice. The elevated design provides growers the ability to improve soil quality and cater to their plants' needs.

Furthermore, it reduces competition between plants by minimizing weeds. Raised beds create a physical barrier between the soil inside and the surrounding ground, preventing weeds from encroaching into the growing area. Start with soil free from weed seeds, use mulch or landscape fabric, and enjoy gardening without having to worry about weed growth. Healthier soil and less competition inevitably lead to bigger harvests. And who doesn't want that?

The raised platform decreases the need to bend or stoop, so long gardening sessions don't leave you feeling exhausted (Trust me, a few years down the road, your back will thank you!).

The reduced risk of pest infestations and soil-borne diseases is another advantage of growing plants in raised beds. The physical barrier keeps the bad guys out while increasing the success rates of targeted treatments. Moreover, your plants get added protection from burrowing animals. Toss in a few rows of fabrics, covers, and cloches and you can rest easy that your harvest will stay protected.

And the best part? You can garden anywhere you like! The versatility in design features means you can choose from a wide variety of materials and adapt according to your needs. If you're into aesthetics, you can use raised beds to give your garden a neat and organized appearance. Get creative and experiment with different materials, shapes, and arrangements to enhance visual appeal.

The size and shape of the bed can be modified based on your plants. For example, deep-rooted crops like potatoes will require a more deep container while a shallow one may suit herbs and salads better. Where you place them is entirely up to you. Over the heavy clay soil in your backyard, in front of that ugly fence, or right on your patio—the options are endless!

In contrast to growing bags or pots, raised beds offer better drainage. This minimizes overwatering and waterlogging. Because the soil is at a higher level from the ground, water is able to drain more easily. The result? You get enough moisture to promote healthy growth while removing excess water. There is a catch, though. Since the soil warms up rather quickly, you may have to water more frequently during the summer or if the bed is placed under harsh sunlight.

The benefits of installing raised beds are too numerous to ignore. These include improved soil quality, better drainage, weed control, extended growing season, flexibility of the design, aesthetic appeal, accessibility, and pest and disease management. If you're looking to increase your garden produce while saving on space, then raised beds are the answer. This simple creation not only leads to healthier plants and increased productivity but makes gardening more enjoyable.

Types of Raised Beds

As long as the design ensures proper drainage, you can get creative juices flowing. Steer clear of harmful materials that may leach into the soil and you're good to go. While there are a vast number of materials for you to choose from, there are three main types of raised beds. These include raised ground beds, supported raised beds, and containerized beds. Each kind has its own benefits, suitable for different outdoor places and plants.

Raised Ground Beds

If you're on a tight budget, then a raised ground bed is the best option for you. These "built-in raised beds" are without frames. They're simple mounds of soil, 6 to 8 inches higher than the surrounding area with a flat top. The exclusion of the frame makes them the most budget-friendly option; however, they do require a larger planting area. They can also be built with a short enclosed frame using bricks, stones, or rot-resistant wood.

The deceptively simple design still offers the same advantages such as good soil drainage and weed prevention. In addition, they provide better accessibility, making planting, weeding, and harvesting feel like a breeze! If you've got a large area to work with and you don't want to skip the process of building a frame, then give them a try.

Supported Raised Beds

These beds include frameworks elevated by legs. Wood, metal, plastic, and stone are usually the materials of choice. They're great for landscaping and sloped backyards as they help create an even surface for planting.

The design allows people with disabilities to garden with ease. Gardeners suffering from knee or back pain may also find it easier to tend to their plants in supported raised beds. They're a great choice for areas with poor soil quality, providing more control over the growing media. Moreover, the elevated frame prevents damage by small animals and insects.

Containerized Raised Beds

These beds make use of pots and barrels to create a contained gardening area. They're quite deep (10 inches or more) and can fit anywhere in your backyard, balcony, or patio. This makes them perfect for people with limited outdoor space. Their portable design makes them a popular option for areas that get variable amounts of sunlight and gardeners looking to experiment with different plant combinations.

Elevated raised beds are another variation of containerized beds with even greater height. While they're built similarly to containerized beds, the walls are comparatively higher. People who prefer gardening while standing up may find them a good fit.

Specialized Raised Beds

These raised beds make use of rather unique materials or methods such as decaying wood, straw bales, or hügelkultur. They can feature climbing trellises, arbors, or pallets. The watering systems also vary greatly ranging from reservoir systems in wicking beds to central indentations in keyhole varieties. We'll discuss specialized raised beds in more detail in Chapter 3. For now, let's take a brief look at some of these.

Straw Bale Gardens

Made with straw bales, fertilizer, and compost, these beds act as a growing medium and container. Each straw bale lasts one season, decomposing and breaking down as the plants near harvest. They can be constructed on any surface such as concrete, paving, or lawn. Using new bales each season minimizes the risk of soil-borne diseases while limiting weed growth.

Pallet Gardens

This eco-friendly option can help cut your work in half. Pallet slats provide gardeners with built-in rows for planting. They also cut out sunlight from reaching the soil other than the rows, preventing weed growth. With these beds, you don't have to go through the hassle of making rows or constantly worry about yanking those pesky weeds.

Moreover, the wooden bars can be used to write the names of the plants, helping you easily identify each variety. Pallet beds require no assembly and are mostly readily available. You can simply upcycle a pallet you already have or pick one from the recycling center and start planting!

Arbors and Trellises

When we think of raised beds, we imagine a horizontal structure. The best thing about raised-bed gardening is that nothing is set in stone, and they can be incredibly versatile. There's something extremely satisfying about neatly planted rows of vegetables. However, if you're short on space, a vertical structure helps solve the problem.

You can train your vegetables on trellises and arbors in the beginning of the season. Within a month or so, you'll find the structure completely transformed by the plant and later by the harvest. You can take down the setup next year or try it somewhere else with another plant.

A standalone or wall-mounted trellis is more suitable for vegetables. Tall, narrow structures that can be set into containers are better for growing smaller plants on decks or patios. Fine materials such as bamboo, lattice, and copper pipes are usually the best options.

Keyhole Gardens

A keyhole garden is a raised circular garden bed with a wedge-shaped indentation on one side, giving the structure the appearance of a keyhole. The cutout makes it easy to access the compost area in the middle and the growing areas on each side. The composting section in the center adds a self-fertilizing element for the plants, naturally replenishing the soil. The soil used in keyhole raised gardens contains special layering to ensure good drainage and increase moisture retention, creating the optimal environment for healthy plant growth.

Self-Watering Wicking Beds

This innovative design is quickly gaining attention worldwide for its efficiency. Essentially, it's simply a large-scale version of a self-watering pot, which has been around for ages.

Figure 1: Self watering container.

It's based on the principle of sub-irrigation, where the water reservoir is right under the pot and reaches the soil through a wick.

Wicking beds are excellent in places where watering is infrequent. The water body can contain enough supply to last several weeks, depending on the location, climate, and season. They're also great for planting around trees, such as Australian eucalyptus, with invasive roots that soak up every last bit of moisture, depriving other smaller plants in the surrounding area.

Hügelkultur

"Hill culture" is the literal translation of the German word used to describe this method. The plants are grown on raised beds that look like mounds. This centuries-old tradition involves building garden beds from plant debris and rotten logs. The woody material is piled up and covered with compost and soil. The mounds can reach an impressive 5 or 6 feet above the ground.

Materials such as cardboard, straw, leaves, manure, grass clippings, and broken branches can be used to make the mound wider at the bottom. Gradually, the wood breaks down and the bed sinks. For example, a mound that is 6 feet high will shrink to 2 feet the following year.

The composting process in hügelbeds generates a considerable amount of heat, warming up the soil and extending the growing season. As the woody material decays, it slowly releases a steady supply of nutrients. The wood also acts like a sponge, storing rainwater and releasing it during times of drought. Moreover, the soil is self-tilling. As the woody material breaks down, it creates tiny air pockets, crumbling the soil.

Key Takeaways

At first glance, raised beds may seem pretty straightforward, but their flexible design makes them remarkably versatile. Their multitude of benefits simply can't be overlooked. From improving soil quality and moisture retention to preventing the spread of disease and keeping out pests, they ensure healthy plant growth every step of the way.

Although every raised bed follows the same principle, they come in various shapes, sizes, and materials. Raised ground beds are the simplest and most economical option available. Supported and containerized beds elevate the planting area, making them the perfect solution for gardening in locations with poor soil. Specialized raised beds make use of innovative techniques such as hügelkultur and self-watering wicking beds. Straw bale, pallet, and keyhole gardens make use of unique frames.

Now that you're well-versed in the basics of raised beds, let's move onto another important aspect of introducing them in your garden. Planning your garden layout is the first and most crucial step in determining your success. So, get a pen and paper ready because it's time to start sketching!

Chapter 2

Planning Your Garden

While a raised bed can go on almost any surface, there are a few factors you should keep in mind when deciding where to place one. A well-planned garden inevitably leads to an abundant harvest. Understanding your growing space is the hallmark of successful gardening. So put on your hat, step into the sun, and start mapping out your garden!

Raised Bed Dimensions: Size Matters!

Length, width, and height are some aspects of raised beds you must keep in mind before designing your garden layout. On average, a raised bed is almost 3 to 4 feet wide and 6 to 10 feet long. These dimensions suit small and large spaces alike, allowing easy access to the crops. If back problems are your concern, then you won't have to strain too hard while caring for your plants. Tasks such as removing weeds, tilling the soil, and water can be performed easily in a bed this size.

Four feet is the ideal size, if you don't have a lot of space. If you intend to place the beds against a fence or a wall, then it'll be best for them to be about 2 to 3 feet wide so you can reach the farthest side with ease. Usually, the height is a minimum of 8 to 12 inches deep. Beds that are 12 to 18 inches deep are mostly used for vegetables. You can increase or decrease the depth based on your preference. Generally, more depth is required when drainage is an issue and the beds are created with a slight slope to avoid standing water.

The height of the raised bed varies depending on the location. For instance, if it's placed on a hard surface, it should be deep enough for the plant roots to form extensive networks. A shallow container only allows the roots to reach the subsoil before hitting the hard surface, which can stunt plant growth.

Another important point to consider, while choosing a raised bed, is that taller frames hold more volume. After watering, the soil becomes rather heavy, placing strain on the structure. If the raised bed is too small, it could gradually start bending outwards with use. In this case, you'll have to install a cross-support at the center to provide additional support.

Now that you have a rough idea of how much space your raised bed will need, let's find a suitable place to put it.

Understanding Your Space and Environment

For a successful harvest, finding the perfect spot for your raised garden bed is key. Start by narrowing down areas in your house that receive a minimum of six hours of direct sunlight. Observe the area for a few days, noting how the surrounding objects cast shadows throughout the day. Aim for a spot that receives unobstructed sunlight.

Placing the bed on a flat surface can enhance accessibility while ensuring easy maintenance. However, avoid low-lying zones at the bottom of hills so water doesn't collect in your garden. Moreover, resist the temptation of placing raised beds next to fences or walls as it can make gardening somewhat cumbersome. Daily gardening tasks will feel much easier if you can access the bed from all sides.

Assessing the microclimates different locations in your garden have to offer should also factor into the decision-making process. Some places may be warmer than others or more humid. Similarly, checking soil drainage is a prerequisite to avoiding waterlogged areas while studying wind patterns can help you protect fragile plants and provide proper air circulation.

Keep it Sunny

Vegetables need several hours of direct sunlight to grow; a minimum of 6 hours is an essential daily requirement. With this in mind, choose an area that soaks up a lot of sun. You can even use Google satellite images to create a map of your potential garden and record the hours of sunlight it receives each day.

Keeping a garden journal can also help you track light and shadow changes on your land. Observe light changes every two hours through the course of a day, noting the places where shadows fall and the number of hours they remain in shade. Remember that bare-branched trees may create the illusion of a sunlit area during autumn, and cast heavy shadows during spring and summer when the leaves come out. Pay close attention to the shadows cast by buildings and walls as you plot the sun's path, as they may change throughout the day. To make tracking even easier, consider using my 'Guided Garden Planner Log Book and Journal,' designed to help you keep detailed records. You'll find a link to it at the end of this book.

You can also use marking flags or stakes to map out light and dark areas or make a light map on paper. Take a few sheets of tracing paper and sketch your yard's outline on each page. Two hours after sunrise, mark down the light and dark areas.

Repeat the process on a new page at different times throughout the day. Stop recording an hour before sunset. With a pencil, mark the sun and shade pockets on each page. Layer the pages together and you'll have an accurate depiction of changing sunlight patterns in your yard.

Well-Draining Soil for the Win

Waterlogged beds are a gardener's worst nightmare. You can avoid running into this disaster by testing the soil for good drainage. Well-draining soil is crucial for growing healthy plants. The last thing you want is for water to pool up at the bottom of your raised bed and lead to root rot.

Start by assessing the soil. Heavy clay soils clump together and lead to compaction. You need soil that is light and crumbles easily in your hand. Amendments such as mulch, sand, or peat moss can alleviate the problem in the raised bed. However, you want to avoid depressed, low-lying areas where water may collect during excess rainfall, so the beds are not surrounded by standing water.

Observe, take note, and steer clear from wet spots such as low-lying areas or the place directly under a downspout. A little trick to help you decide your raised bed's location in your backyard is to pay attention to what's growing there currently. Do you see a tuft of grass? Does it look healthy and green? If so, then you may just have found the perfect spot for growing your vegetables. If mosses or swampy looking tall grasses are what you see, then they could be an indication of excess moisture or shade.

If the landscape around you is mostly flat and you want your garden on a hilly site, then make sure to position the growing beds perpendicular to the direction of the slope. This way, the soil will not get washed away when the water flows downhill. For an area with a steep incline, terracing the landscape can help prevent soil erosion.

Easy Breezy

To maintain the best growing conditions for your plants, you need to ensure that fresh air circulates through the growing space. Place the beds in an open area where old air is naturally flushed out. A continuous stream of fresh air helps distribute the moisture evenly while keeping the temperature in check.

Good air circulation helps maintain the ideal humidity and temperature for plants, ensuring an optimal growing environment. Too much moisture in the air could lead to mold and fungal diseases and cause the plants to become stretched and limp.

While stagnant air is usually not an issue for outdoor gardening, it's best to allow sufficient space between the beds and surrounding structures to maintain adequate air flow. Avoid overcrowding by planting the crops too close to each other as this could cause moisture build-up and increase the risk of fungal diseases.

Finally, avoid extremely windy areas or place the beds near a fence or hedge for shelter. Strong gusts of wind can damage delicate plants and dry out the soil more quickly. It's best to observe wind patterns in your area and position the beds in a place that offers protection from fierce wind storms while ensuring proper air circulation.

Water

A convenient and consistent water supply could determine the success, or failure, of your raised garden bed. However, before placing the bed near an outdoor faucet and considering the job done, consider the overall practicality of the location. Sometimes your yard may not be the best choice for your growing beds even though it seems logical. Make sure the bed is not only close to an outdoor faucet but also accessible with a garden hose, so you can water with ease.

A drip irrigation system could help you increase your watering efficiency. The method ensures even watering while streamlining the process and minimizing water loss. Make sure your chosen location offers adequate water pressure for watering through irrigation systems and hoses.

Soaker hoses offer a cost-effective alternative to drip irrigation. Consider using these if you're working with a tight budget to deliver water directly to the soil surrounding your plants. Rain barrels are also a smart, eco-friendly solution during dry spells, so consider incorporating these in your setup. Finally, keep a close eye on soil moisture or invest in moisture sensors to estimate water needs for your raised bed. Ideally, you should water your plants when the top soil dries out about an inch. Watering too frequently or sparingly can adversely affect your plants.

Logistics

Keep logistics in mind while designing your garden layout. Ensure your garden offers easy access for maintenance purposes and transport of materials such as compost and garden waste. The beds should be positioned at a comfortable height to ensure easy planting, harvesting, and watering.

Placing the bed near the door in the backyard could make it easier for you to check on your plants than if it's hidden at the far end. Keeping the growing bed close to the house will also encourage you to visit your plants more frequently. As they say, "the best fertilizer for plants is the gardener's shadow." So make sure you don't leave your plants unattended for too long.

The tool shed, water valve and other necessary supplies should be in close proximity to your garden. You don't want to end up carrying heavy water buckets over long distances. A garden hose that easily reaches your growing bed is a convenient option for watering. Your garden layout should be designed in a way that maximizes productivity and makes gardening easier. A little foresight could make your gardening experience more pleasant and avoid running into problems.

Garden Layout: Making Everything Fit

It's time to piece the puzzle! Here are some factors you need to consider before deciding on the final placement of your raised bed:

Getting the Size Right

As we discussed above, an average raised bed ranges from 3 to 4 feet wide and 6 to 10 feet long. The size fits small and large spaces alike, allowing easy access so you don't have to strain too much to get rid of the weeds, till the soil, or water your beloved greens. A width of 4 feet is ideal, if you can only make room for one.

When set against a wall or a fence, a width of 2 to 3 feet is best so you can access the farthest sides. A depth of 12 to 18 inches is preferred for growing vegetables. You can increase the depth, if you're concerned about drainage or simply opt for a porous growing medium. An inclination of about 2% to prevent the risk of standing water.

A major concern for most gardeners is to minimize the need to step inside the bed. This is why being able to reach the plants from all sides is so important. A width of 3 feet is usually best for children while adults easily manage 4 feet. For wheelchair access, a width of 2 feet for children and 3 feet for adults is ideal.

Although the length of the bed is not as important as the width, very long raised beds could prove to be rather difficult to walk and work around. Moreover, the materials used could impact how long your raised bed turns out to be. Since the cost of lumber increases considerably above 12 feet, it's best to keep the length well under that figure.

The ideal height for raised beds is around 10 inches. The more you increase the height, the more soil you'll need to fill it up. Being mindful of the cost and labor involved this might entail could help you decide the appropriate height for your raised beds. For wheelchair access, you can go for 10-inch-deep raised planters elevated on legs or blocks to reach a comfortable height of 24 inches. This will create the perfect height for people with disabilities to garden with comfort while saving up on soil.

Garden crops usually require a minimum 10 inches of soil. If the height of your raised bed is lower than this, then you may have to till the ground underneath. If the bed is over a hard surface, 10 inches may not be deep enough for vegetables like potatoes.

In the end, the overall dimensions of the raised beds depend on your available space, gardening targets, and practical considerations. The number of plants that you intend to grow, crop rotation schemes, and accessibility should all factor into the decision making process. While the ideal size remains 3 to 4 feet wide and 6 to 10 feet in length, sketch this into your garden layout and don't be afraid to make any necessary adjustments based on the above reasons.

Wall Thickness

The thickness of the walls largely depends on the material used. For instance, a layer of recycled concrete block that's 8-inches thick will take up more space and increase the width of the raised bed. Meanwhile, lumber of 1-inch thickness requires vertical support every 4 feet in length.

Walkways

Include at least one central path in your garden layout that stretches from one end to the other. Other walkways should merge with the main pathway, allowing you to move with ease. In a large sized garden, you can add multiple paths that are wide enough for you to move small equipment like wheelbarrows or carry heavy items such as bags of soil or fertilizer.

The paths should connect each bed, allowing you to move around them easily. A width of 12 inches between the beds is ideal in a small space where a lot of gardeners won't be working at the same time. For more comfortable access, you may have to build the paths 18 to 24 inches wide and space the beds 4 feet from each other.

Orientation

If you're left with adequate space between the beds, then orientation may not be a problem. Tall plants will naturally provide shade to the smaller crops, if planted in the same bed. When plants are growing in separate beds with little space between them, planting on an east-west orientation may cause taller plants in one bed to cause shadows on smaller plants in another. Positioning the beds in a north-south direction can help you avoid this.

Irrigation

Give careful thought to the irrigation system you plan to use while planning your layout. Drip irrigation is usually a lot easier to install when the beds are positioned in a straight line or any other orderly pattern.

Garden layout usually doesn't impact the installation process of overhead sprinklers; however, for maximum results position the beds in circular, square, or rectangular patterns. Finally, keeping the space between the beds uniform throughout the garden will make hand watering with a hose a lot easier.

Shape

While figuring out the location of your planting beds, you may want to consider the shape of the arrangement. Based on what you're looking for, you can include raised beds of different kinds such as wood, metal, brick, stone, straw bales, or plant directly in the ground. Group together large containers or go for self-watering planters. Aesthetics come into play when you've made the big decisions. Common design patterns for raised garden beds include the following

- *Rectangle*
  Gives the garden a neat, organized look with visible paths and beds. The arrangement offers an efficient design that maximizes the planting area and space utilization. May not be ideal for sloping sites.
- *L-shaped*
  Splits the garden into distinct areas, offering a lot of variety with the placement of the beds.
- *Triangle*
  Excellent for making use of the corners, but may not be a good choice for an inclined area.
- *Circle*
  The central path could cut across the middle of the circle with herbs and small leafy vegetables as the centerpiece. It's an aesthetically pleasing option, best for flat surfaces.

Irregular

An irregular arrangement suits beds that are deep. The paths carve out the shape and can be used as the borders. The design works best on sloped areas.

Maximize Space Through Vertical Structures

Space is usually limited in an urban setting, but it shouldn't stop you from growing your own food. Thinking out of the box and trying different settings helps you incorporate the maximum number of plants in small areas. Vertical gardening provides an innovative solution for growers struggling with space constraints.

Trellises, arbors, and stakes not only enhance your garden's aesthetic appeal but also help optimize space utilization. For example, you can install trellises or lattice panels to the sides of your raised beds to support climbing plants like tomatoes and peas.

Choosing the Right Plants

The success of your vertical garden and its aesthetic appeal depend largely on the plants you choose. Plants compatible with the unique microenvironment of your garden have a better chance of surviving and thriving in vertical spaces.

Consider factors such as climate, watering requirements, and growth patterns while you're at the gardening center. Herbs like basil, parsley, and mint adapt well to growing in vertical spaces as do small vegetables such as lettuce and spinach. Creepers like cherry tomatoes and peas not only grow well on trellises and stakes, but offer stunning visuals as well.

Types of Vertical Gardens

You can let your imagination loose when it comes to vertical gardening. Growing plants "upward" can be achieved in a number of ways. Here are some kinds of vertical gardening structures that you can include in your layout:

1. **Wall-mounted Planters**

    Make use of bare walls by mounting your pots and planters. They can be a great place for your herbs, succulents, and other small plants.

2. **Trellis Systems**

    Perfect for climbing plants such as beans, cucumbers, and peas, they can either be constructed with wood or metal, attached to a wall or left freestanding.

3. **Green Walls**

   Made up of plants that grow soil or soilless medium, they work well both indoors and outdoors.

4. **Pallet Garden**

   Repurpose old wooden pallets with some landscape fabric attached to the back and fix it to a wall. Fill it up with a potting mix and start planting!

5. **Hanging Pocket Planters**

   Made with upcycled materials, such as plastic bottles or canvas shoe organizers, the planters are attached to a wall or fence to create an inexpensive vertical garden.

6. **Ladder Shelving**

   Repurpose an old ladder into a stunning vertical display for your potted plants.

Planning and Design

Careful planning and design are crucial for a successful vertical garden. Depending on the space available, resources required, and personal taste, you can build a beautiful yet functional vertical garden. The first step, as always, is finding the perfect spot for your vertical structure.

Keep available sunlight, other environmental factors and accessibility for maintenance in mind while making our decision. If a suitable wall in the garden or a sunny spot on the patio checks all the requirements for the plant you want to grow, in addition to the points above, then go for it!

You've a wide variety of structures to choose from, including modular planter systems, repurposed pallets, and wall-mounted containers. They may require a customized irrigation system for efficient watering. Drip irrigation or self-watering containers can ensure consistent watering of the plants growing vertically, with minimal wastage.

Maintenance

With proper maintenance you can make your vertical gardens flourish. Plants growing vertically need more frequent watering because of their shallow root systems and exposed soil. Keep a close eye on moisture levels and water as needed. In addition to this, regular feedings with liquid fertilizer or slow-release granules will ensure your plants continue growing optimally.

Trimming overgrowth and removing dead leaves through routine pruning will encourage healthy new growth while maintaining aesthetic appeal. The plants in your vertical garden may be more vulnerable to pests and disease, so look for signs of problems and treat them early on.

Vertical gardens offer an innovative solution for space constraints. By utilizing vertical spaces, urban gardeners can bring nature into their small homes transforming it into a thriving oasis.

Key Takeaways

Planning the layout marks the first step toward building a flourishing raised garden bed. Start by deciding the size of your raised bed and analyze your gardening space to find the perfect spot. Sunlight, water, soil, air circulation, and logistics play key roles in the success of your garden bed.

Once you've found a suitable location, you can focus on other design elements and add in more features. Add in walkways and paths and orient your raised beds to improve drainage and increase or decrease access to sunlight. Experiment with different arrangements and work your irrigation system into the design to avoid running into problems later.

If you're struggling with limited space, then start growing your plants upward. Vertical gardens not only serve stunning visuals, but help maximize space. There are various upright structures for you to choose from ranging from green walls to ladder shelving. With proper maintenance and care, you can keep your plants flourishing for a long time. Include trellises, arbors, and green walls in your layout and add multiple layers to your raised garden bed.

With the blueprints ready, let's roll up our sleeves and move onto the heavy lifting. Chapter 3 is all about bringing your raised garden bed to life. Time to put your DIY skills to the test and turn your home into paradise!

Chapter 3

How to Build A Raised Garden Bed

You can let your imagination soar when it comes to raised beds, building them in any shape, size, or material you like. Make your garden above the ground in metal, stone, wood, animal troughs, canoes or, even, wine bottles! There are no limits to what you can create.

One thing you must keep in mind, before deciding your material of choice, is durability. Generally, the more the material costs, the more long-lasting it tends to be. When on a budget, you can upcycle to bring down the cost without compromising on quality or scavenge good-quality supplies.

Regardless of where you source the material, your raised beds must fulfill certain criteria. They should be durable, accessible, easy to work with and safe to use. Let's explore some options of sustainable materials for making raised beds.

Selecting the Right Materials

Some factors to consider while choosing your material include cost, availability, suitability to your climate, and whether you plan to stay put or move around. Here are some options for you to consider:

Untreated Wood

Rot resistant wood options such as cypress, redwood, and cedar, which are not only durable but also free from harsh chemicals that could potentially leach into the soil. Milled wood planks may be sturdy but tend to deteriorate within a few years.

Logs, branches, and sticks are a possible alternative to wooden boards and cost less. Scavenging the wood around your area is an environmentally-friendly and cost-effective option that you can explore. When piled up, the logs and branches can create a vertical frame around the perimeter of the bed. Another option is to weave long, slender branches into a wattle fence to surround your raised garden.

Plastic and Resin

Plastic and resin beds have garnered much attention in recent years. For one, they're easily available and usually come fully assembled or with user-friendly manuals. These reasons alone make them the most popular for raised beds.

The modular design makes them convenient and fairly simple to set up. Some varieties are propped up on legs, bringing greater comfort to the gardening experience. Moreover, the beds are long-lasting, so you won't have to worry about replacing or repairing after each growing season.

Most plastic and resin beds available in the market today are BPA-free and made with polyethylene, eliminating the risk of harmful chemicals leaching into the soil. Furthermore, most varieties are recyclable, making them relatively eco-friendly options.

A crucial point to remember with plastic beds is that, unless you're using a specifically BPA-free variety, some reused and upcycled materials can contain BPA. This means you run the risk of toxic chemicals leaching into the soil and making their way into your food supply. Additionally, some plastics may be advertised as recyclable, but their fate depends on the capability of your municipality's recycling system.

Excessive moisture retention is another issue that you may encounter with plastic beds. This may pose a problem for plants requiring constant drainage. Without sizable drainage holes at the bottom, such plants may not survive in plastic containers.

Metal

Galvanized steel has resurged in both indoor and outdoor accessories. Of these metal raised beds make a new addition. The galvanizing process lends the material to being weather-proof and rust-proof, making it perfect for farms and homesteads. Corrugated galvanized steel, a steel sheet with a ridged pattern, proves particularly sturdy and rigid for raised beds. It's lightweight, too, making construction easier.

A powder coating provides an additional protective layer, increasing durability. Applied in liquid form, the process involves coating the metal surface with dry powder with a special gun to give the powder a negative charge. As a result the powder particles are attracted to the metal, evenly coating the material without dripping. The metal is heated later on to bind the particles together, creating a smooth, long lasting finish, resistant to chips and scratches. Aluminum trough planters are also an excellent choice, offering a rust-proof option. Impervious to rust by nature, aluminum is ideal for landscape use

Bricks and Stones

If you've got plenty of natural stone on your land (and a strong back), then you can build beautiful raised beds that last ages. Flagstones and mossy rocks are some good options. While scavenging, look for stones with flat surfaces, as these can be stacked easily, rather than round, smooth stones commonly found in most places. Granite, fieldstone, sandstone, limestone, flagstone, basalt, slate, and cobblestone are some examples of natural stones that you can use.

Bricks, made from clay baked at high temperatures, are easy to stack, making them great for raised beds. However, they require some heavy lifting and may not offer the same aesthetic appeal as wood or stone.

Straw Bales

It's best to go for real straw and not hay. Made from oat, wheat, or alfalfa, straw bales don't contain a lot of seeds. This is due to the fact that straw is harvested following the removal of grain and chaff. On the other hand, hay is usually packed full of seeds that will sprout and invade your crops. However, avoid pine straw because its waterproof pine needles may prevent water retention.

Although the straw provides the plants with some nutrients while it decomposes, it can't replace the need for good garden soil. This makes the addition of some fertilizer and frequent watering a must. How long the bales last depends largely on your climate. Generally, they stay good for two to four years.

Fabric

Using grow bags or fabric beds comes with plenty of advantages and only a few downsides. They can be assembled in various configurations, fitting almost any space. They come in different sizes, ranging from 5 gallons to 100, so you can build your new garden or expand an existing one.

They're especially great for small spaces like balconies or patios. They don't leave stains on concrete surfaces and most plants respond well to them. They're easy to move around, allowing you to move your plants indoors during winter or change their position in the garden.

However, bigger grow bags tend to be much bulkier and difficult to move around. They don't retain moisture very well and you may find yourself watering too frequently. In particularly hot or cold weather, you may have to add a heavy layer of mulch to prevent them from drying out.

Five Materials to Avoid

Now that we've discussed the materials perfect for making raised beds, let's look at what not to use:

1. Railroad Ties

Their funky-cool appearance may seem tempting at first, but these blocks of woods are treated with creosote—a possible carcinogen. Besides posing a risk to your health, it can also inhibit or damage your plants.

2. Pressure Treated Wood

Gardeners tend to have divided opinions on this one. In the past, an arsenic-based compound known as chromated copper arsenate (CCA) was used to cure pressure treated lumber. Arsenic leaches into the soil and could harm the plants.

The purpose of using CCA was to make cheaper wood varieties, like pine, last longer. In 2003, CCA was banned and replaced with less-toxic copper based chemicals such as alkaline copper quaternary (ACQ).

Although ACQ is relatively less toxic, high concentrations of copper can leach into the soil and make its way to water sources, harming aquatic life. So it's better to avoid treated lumber altogether. Moreover, redwood and cedar outlast pressure treated pine by a number of years, so why risk exposing your plants to toxic material?

3. MB Pallets

Wood pallets offer a cost-effective and eco-friendly solution; however, avoid the ones stamped with "MB," methyl bromide. A broad spectrum pesticide, MB can be extremely harmful to your health. While they may help eliminate fungi, roundworms, insects, and rodents, MB pallets are incredibly damaging for the ozone layer.

When choosing a pallet for your raised bed—or any DIY project—go for the ones stamped with "HT," which stands for heat treated. These are sterilized for a minimum of 30 minutes at 132°F or more, making them a safe upcycling option.

4. Cinder Blocks

Constructed with fly ash or coal particles, cinder blocks may contain traces of arsenic, mercury, lead, or other heavy metals. Even though they haven't been mass produced in almost half a century, it's best to entirely rule them out as a construction material for your raised bed. Present-day concrete blocks look identical to cinder blocks of the heyday, but are built from Portland cement and other aggregates. Concrete is generally considered non-toxic and safe for plants.

5. Old Tires

While turning old tires into beautiful and useful things is truly commendable, it's better to avoid them in the garden. They contain cadmium and lead along with a number of other toxic materials that could leach into the soil.

Some believe that tires shed most of the toxins within the first year of use. So far, no research has been performed to determine whether old tires contaminate soil, following use in the garden, or not. Still, it's better to be safe than sorry and avoid them, if possible.

Tips for Choosing the Right Material

Confused about what materials you can use for your raised bed? Here are a few tips to help you make the best decision.

Keep It Natural

The goal is to build an organic environment as close to their natural state as possible. For example, untreated wood, steel that isn't coated with chemicals and stones that haven't been chemically altered.

Make Sure It's Durable

Your raised garden beds will go through all kinds of weather over the years. So choose materials that'll stand the test of time. When it comes to longevity, untreated wood is your best bet. Cedar, redwood, hemlock, and cypress can extend your raised garden bed's lifespan by almost a decade. Next in line is steel followed by stones and concrete.

Choose your material wisely for a stress-free gardening experience with minimum requirement for repairs.

Keep Aesthetics In Mind

If you're confused about aesthetics, pick materials that complement your landscape. Assess the feel and style of your home then choose materials that complement that style. If you're looking for something to add a touch of sophistication to go with your stucco home, then you may want to try wooden beds, wrought iron arbors and furniture with curlicue patterns to create a French feel.

Stand outside and look at your home. How would you describe the architecture and feel of the space? Is it modern? Traditional? Or mediterranean? You can also google different elements of your home to find accurate words to describe its present style. Look up your homes' construction materials, unique architectural features, roof or ceiling design or even the year it was built. For example, stucco walls, ornate iron elements, and clay roof tiles are usually the features of a Spanish colonial home. Once you have an accurate description of your home, you can follow the same theme to design your raised garden bed.

Keep it Sound and Sustainable

At the end of the day, upcycling remains the best option. Still, sometimes buying raw materials for your garden is unavoidable. In this case, sustainability should always be in the back of your mind while shopping. When buying hardwood, look for companies that replant trees after each harvest. For metal, such as steel, look up how far the material has traveled and how it was excavated. For stone, go for the ones naturally found in your area.

Keep It Budget Friendly

Affordability is a major concern for most small-scale gardeners, especially if you plan to construct several raised beds. Cedar can be expensive but its incredible longevity makes it worth the cost.

Steel comes in second in terms of affordability while stone gardens built with cement footers tend to be the most expensive. If you're undecided about building a full-scale kitchen garden, try something less permanent and cost-effective like clay pots or fabric grow bags, which remain the most affordable options.

DIY Wooden Raised Beds

When all the prep work is done, it's time to bring out the toolbox and start building! Here's everything you'll need to construct your own raised bed:

Equipment Required

- Hand drill
- Bolt tightener
- Tape measure
- Framing square (optional)
- Pencil
- Saw

Supplies

- Untreated cedar boards:

  2'' Thickness

  6'' Height

  8' Length

Make sure the boards are straight with no chips or cracks

You can ask the store owners to cut them in half to make eight 4' boards.

Here are the steps you need to follow to create the best raised bed for your plants:

Step 1: Measure the boards

Measure the thickness of the wooden boards. Hardware stores usually insist they're 2 inches thick when they're often not. For instance, if your board turns out to be 1 ¾ inches thick, mark it along both edges of all four plants so you create a straight line (this marks the place where the tip of the other board will lie flat against this one). Also, remember that the side you're marking will face the inside of the raised bed.

Step 2: Mark the framing angles

Time to line up the framing angle along the line you just made and mark 2 or 3 holes on the inside. The number depends on how many hex screws you want to use for each side. These are the places where you'll drill, so avoid marking in between two boards. Also, be sure each board has at least one hole. Don't forget to double check the marks! Keep the old adage "Measure twice, cut once," in mind.

Step 3: Drill

Drill each hole in place, making sure to keep it straight.

Step 4: Attach the framing angles

Time to create the panels by attaching each framing angle with hex screws on the outside, washer and nut on the inside. You should end up with two complete panels, secured in place with framing angles.

Step 5: Move onto the other sides

Move onto the other boards. Line them up along the framing angle already fixed to the panel, making sure the edges are straight. Start marking the drilling holes on the two new boards.

Step 6: Finish the first raised bed corner

Take out the boards and drill the holes in the marked places. Fasten the boards to the framing angle using hex screws, washers, and nuts, like above. Congratulations, you now have the first corner of your raised garden bed all ready!

Step 7: Finish the second corner

Repeat the same process: line up two planks, mark the holes, drill, fasten the two boards using screws, washers, and nuts.

Step 8: Check angles

Make sure to check the angles of your U-shaped bed as you go along. You want them to be flush and 90 degrees exact. You can also use a framing square to help you double check.

Step 9: Attach the final panel

Make holes to fasten the last panel to the U-shaped bed. Lay down the U-shaped structure and slide in the final panel after attaching the framing angles. Assemble the final raised bed piece and you're almost done!

Make sure all the bolts are screwed tight. As an extra precaution, go back and tighten each bolt with a bolt tightener once each angle is secured. With all the bolts secured, move your newly constructed bed to your desired spot, fill it up with soil and start growing!

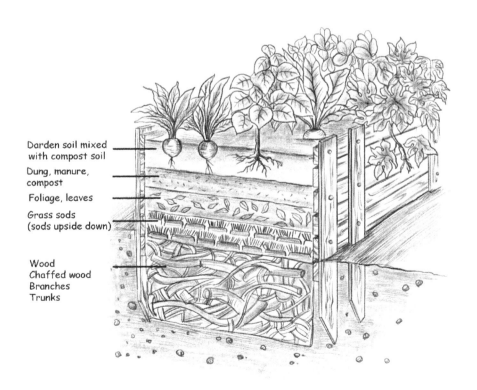

Figure 2: Raised bed filling layers.

Figure 3: DIY grow crates with adjustable wall height.

DIY Cold Frame for Raised Beds

A cold frame can help your vegetables and herbs survive harsh winter conditions. They are also traditionally used to harden off plants grown indoors or in a greenhouse in spring, before planting out into the ground or final containers. Cold frames are themselves like tiny greenhouse allowing sunlight through a transparent top, which keeps the temperature warm. This traps the heat inside, keeping your plants warm and protected. Moreover, plants enclosed in a cold frame don't need to be watered as often, as the box retains a high level of moisture.

You can either buy a commercial cold frame or build one with pieces of wood. For the base, you can use any wooden boxes you may have lying around the house, such as wine boxes. Alternatively, you can join planks to make rectangular structures. Stack these frames on top of each other until the structure matches your plant's height.

For the last frame, we need to create a slope. Cut one of the planks lengthwise to half its width—this will be attached to the front of the rectangle. Measure the width of the plank. Use the measurement to mark a spot for a cut on one end of the two planks that will make the sides. With the help of the dots, make a diagonal line and saw along this line, creating a slope. Finally, nail the planks together.

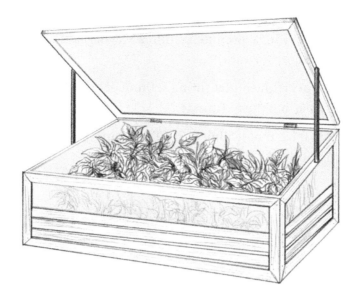

Figure 4: DIY cold frames elongate the growing season.

You can cover the frame with transparent plastic or glass. Depending on your preference, you can either balance the sheet of plastic or glass on top or attach it with hinges. The latter will give the plants more protection, especially during thunderstorms, if your cold frame lies in an area that isn't sheltered. Lastly, lining the base with plastic can help maintain moisture levels by collecting run-off.

DIY Wicking Beds

Let's round up all the tools required to construct your very own wicking bed.

Supplies

- Prefabricated galvanized steel raised bed/ DIY timber raised bed
- Butyl rubber pond liner
- Coarse grade scoria

- Geotextile fabric (15 cm or 6'')

- Soil mix (50% premium soil, 25% organic compost, 25% organic cow manure)

- Water overflow outlet fitting (20mm or ¾'' threaded tank inlet known as bulkhead fitting)

- Water inlet pipe (50mm, 2'' PVC pipe joined by 90 degree elbow joint)

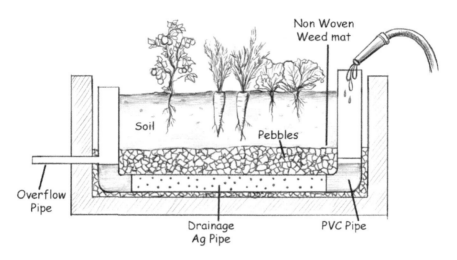

Figure 5: A simple wicked bed construction.

Equipment Required

- Drill

- Spirit level

- Small spring clamps or screw clamps

- Scissors

Once you've got all the supplies ready, it's time to get down to business. In this guide, we'll be working with a galvanized steel raised bed as the base. Here is a step-by-step manual for your DIY wicking bed:

Step 1: Raised bed placement

Place your raised bed in its preferred location. The soil will weigh it down later, making it immovable, so choose wisely.

Step 2: Level the area

Make sure the ground is level using a spirit level. Place it crossways and length-ways at different angles to ensure that the surface is even. This step is particularly important because one side of the wicking bed will become drier than the other on an uneven surface.

Lift the side that's low by packing it with soil. If a spot seems higher than the rest, take some soil out to lower it.

Step 3: Start drilling

Make holes on the sides of the beds, approximately 20 cm (8'') above the ground, using a 20mm hole saw.

Step 4: Bring out the pond liner

Spread the pond liner inside the bed, making sure it fits. As long as it sits well above the scoria layer, minor mismeasuring is okay. The liner doesn't have to reach all the way to the top. It's workable even if it falls short in some places.

Step 5: Fix in place the 20 mm threaded pipe outlet.

Make a hole in the liner with your scissors, big enough for the 20 mm bulkhead connector to pass through. Keep rubber washers of the fitting on the inside, opposite the pond liner, to maintain a watertight seal.

Step 6: Get the water inlet pipes ready

Drill a 10mm (⅜'') holes around the circumference of the 50 mm (2'') wide PVC pipe at least 30 cm (12'') away from one end. The pipe's length should be high enough to allow efficient watering without coming in the way of the plants to find the inlet.

Create holes on the lower side of the water inlet pipe, if you're using a single, straight pipe. Drill along the length of the other pipe, provided that you're using an L-shaped inlet pipe. In the case that you're working with the more common L-shaped water inlet design, use two pipes and join them with an elbow joint.

The horizontal part should be at least half to three quarters the length of the bed, with 10 - 12 mm (⅜'' - ½'') holes all around and along its length. Attach both pipes with the elbow joint, using a friction-fit.

Step 7: Apply a thin layer of coarse scoria on top of the pond liner

This will hold it down, giving it an added layer of protection. Without this protective layer, the liner can get damaged by the PVC inlet pipe. Make sure to layer an adequate amount (5 cm or 2") of scoria, packing it down gently between the pipe's end and the pond liner to prevent puncturing it.

Step 8: Fasten the liner to the garden bed

Fix the pond liner to the top edges of the raised bed with small spring or screw clamps. This will keep it in place while you fill the bed with the remaining scoria and soil.

Step 9: Add coarse scoria

Pour coarse scoria in the bed until it reaches the overflow outlet. Make sure the layer is level and evenly distributed.

Step 10: Place geotextile over the scoria layer

Wrap the fabric well around the inlet pipe, allowing it to cover the pipe to keep out soil and the scoria layer. Apply at least two layers of the fabric. Alternatively, you can also use a single layer of thick shade cloth, tucked in, and pushed down the sides between the liner and the scoria.

Remember that for your wicking bed to work, the edges need to dip into the water, wicking it upward. Secure the geotextile layer by tucking it in around the sides, where the pond liner touches the scoria along the walls. This will leave a narrow, wedge-shaped space down the side, allowing some soil to fill it up. Keep in mind that the soil is required for the wicking, not the scoria. A part of the fabric with the soil folded inside it must dip into the water, acting as a 'wick.'

Step 10: Level the scoria layer

Pat down any bumps and raise low spots by pressing the sides to fill in the hollow in the middle. If the layer's surface is too irregular, lift a part of the fabric, level the scoria, then put it back in place.

Step 11: Fill up the raised bed with soil

After making sure that the liner is pressed flat against the walls, start filling the bed with the soil mix. When you're done, check the blue plastic pot on the top of the water inlet. This acts as a cap to keep out dirt and debris, preventing it from entering the water reservoir.

Step 12: Trim the excess pond liner

Leaving 3 cm (1- ¼ ''), snip off the excess liner with a pair of scissors.

Step 13: Water the soil

We're almost near the finish line, it's time to water the bed and start planting! Moisten the soil, pouring water until it reaches the scoria layer. Use the inlet pipe to fill the water reservoir, allowing the excess to flow out the overflow pipe. Plant up, apply some mulch, then sit back and let your wicking raised bed do all the work!

DIY Barrel Planters

Ever thought about upcycling plastic barrels for planters? You'll be surprised by how effective they are in helping you cut back on space. Empty plastic barrels can be easily turned into vertical planters for small plants. Ideally, a 55-gallon (200 liter) plastic drum barrel is a good choice. Clean the barrel thoroughly and make 5-inch (12.7 cm) slits by using a knife or drill. You will plant the seedlings in these openings. Prepare a PVC pipe by poking 0.5 - 1 inch (1- 2.5 cm) holes along its entire length. This will serve as an irrigation system, providing water to the plants.

Figure 6: Strawberries are thriving in barrel planters.

Don't forget to create a few drainage holes at the bottom of the barrel. Fill the planter with soil and insert a PVC pipe in the center, which will supply water to the plants. Sprinkle the seeds in the slits or transplant the seedlings. These planters are perfect for herbs, chilies, strawberries and other small plants.

DIY Hügelkultur Beds

Here's everything you need to build a hügelkultur bed in your garden:

Supplies

- Wood:
    - ✓ Large-sized pieces for the bottom

- ✓ Medium-sized pieces for the top
- ✓ Small pieces for the third layer (optional)
- ✓ Choose hardwood trees and conifers

Avoid cedar because it can take a considerably long time to break down

Use a mix of fresh and old wood to provide your plants with a consistent supply of nutrients

Avoid willow and black lotus which can sprout easily

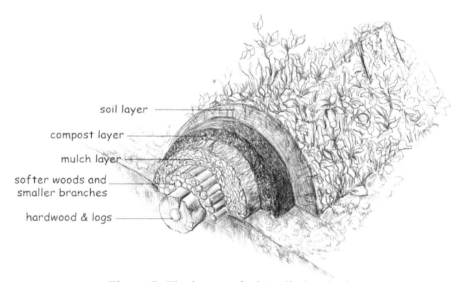

soil layer

compost layer

mulch layer

softer woods and smaller branches

hardwood & logs

Figure 7: The layers of a hügelkultur bed.

Step 1: Start piling up

Start building your hügelkultur bed by stacking large logs and branches on the area you've chosen for your hügelkultur bed. Leave small gaps, approximately 2 - 3 inches or 5 - 8 cm, between each piece. This will allow the soil to trickle down into the bed later.

While laying down the wood, keep the width a bit less than what you ultimately intend for the bed. This is because the width of the bed will increase after the addition of soil and mulch.

Make sure the wood pile is not too narrow, or the sides will end up becoming too steep. This can cause the soil, and mulch, to roll down the sides when you add them later. You want the bed to give the appearance of a mound rather than a pyramid.

Step 2: Add the first layer of soil

Start adding the soil, and filling in the gaps between the wood pieces. Cover the sides first then move onto the top.

If you like you can add manure or other nitrogen-rich material at this stage. However, avoid fresh animal manure as it could burn the roots.

Step 3: Place medium-sized wood

Once the large pieces are buried in the soil, start adding the medium sized pieces. They should be comparatively smaller than the wood used earlier, but still big enough. Remember the goal is to create a mound, not a pyramid so leave some gaps on the sides of each piece.

Step 4: Apply second layer of soil

Add a thick layer of soil and compost. Avoid using manure at this point as the young plant's roots will quickly penetrate into this level. Some gardeners add a third layer of small wood pieces. Personally, I think the additional layer makes little difference and can make planting a little difficult.

Usually, an additional layer doesn't create problems as long as you're planting with seeds. However, you may want to reconsider this step if you plan to transplant your plants. In the absence of a third layer of small wood pieces, the mixture of soil and compost you just applied becomes your final layer. As a result, it should be the thickest of them all, ranging between 4 to 6 inches (10 to 15 cm).

Step 5: Top the bed with mulch

A nice, thick layer of mulch adds the final touches to our hügelkultur bed. You can use a layer of fall leaves along with wood chips. Although these beds are excellent at water retention, they eventually dry out. The müulch layer helps the soil trap moisture in the soil.

The thickness of the final mulch layer should be at least 2 inches (5cm). However, if the sides are too steep, some of the mulch may roll down and you may need to add more to the top.

*Sunken Hügelkultur Bed

The steps above apply to simple Hügelkultur beds; however, many variations exist. In sunken hügelkultur beds, the bed is partially buried. These beds are much better at retaining moisture, making them a great choice for extremely dry climates like the American southwest.

To construct this, you need to dig a trench before following step 1. The rest of the process follows the same steps mentioned above. You just have to keep going until the bed reaches ground level. At this stage, you can create a little mound, if you like, or leave it be.

DIY Lasagna Bed

Lasagna gardening involves minimal physical labor. With no tilling or digging required, you can easily construct a lasagna bed and enjoy the benefits of rich, fluffy soil, teeming with helpful microorganisms. The result: healthier plants, fewer pests, higher yields, and fewer weeds.

As the name suggests, lasagna gardening refers to a method in which different layers of organic matter are allowed to "cook" over time. We've discussed this method in detail in my book *The Practical Permaculture Project*. The process creates healthy soil, fit for growing healthy, robust crops.

Figure 8: Lasagna bed layers.

Let's look at the materials required to build a lasagna bed:

Equipment Required

- A shovel

Supplies

- Grass clippings
- Leaves
- Fruit and vegetable scraps
- Coffee grounds
- Tea bags or tea leaves
- Manure
- Compost
- Seaweed
- Shredding newspaper
- Pine needles
- Garden trimmings
- Peat moss
- Cardboard

Step 1: Build the frame

Generally, this should be around 4 x 8 feet which is 2 to 3 feet high. However, you can adjust the dimensions according to the space available in your backyard. If the soil quality on your property isn't great then you can use a layer of landscape fabric to prevent roots from penetrating the ground. Follow the steps for a DIY wooden raised bed above to create a standard wooden bed.

Step 2: Get the area ready

With a square-point shovel level the soil, pressing down the bumps and filling in the holes. Don't stress too much about the grass or weeds as these will get covered up later. Measure and mark your area according to the dimensions of the bed you're planning.

Step 3: Round up the materials

Time to go for a stroll around the neighborhood or your own backyard. Start collecting materials required for your lasagna bed such as leaves, fallen flowers, grass, or cardboard pieces.

Step 4: Start layering

Create a thick cardboard or newspaper layer. This will act as ground cover, preventing the weeds from sprouting. Eventually, it'll completely decompose, adding nutrients to your soil.

Step 5: Add the second layer

Add water-absorbent materials like dried grass, straw or bark. This will ensure good drainage. Break twigs, small branches or gardening trimmings into 1 inch pieces and create a 4 inch layer on top of the cardboard.

Step 6: Add a third layer

Composed of organic materials, the third layer should range between 4 to 8 inches in thickness. This layer only contains organic materials such as grass clippings and compost.

Step 7: Add the remaining layers

Repeat the layers until the bed is approximately 2 feet tall. As the different layers begin decomposing, the bed will gradually shrink.

Step 8: Water

Pour water to kickstart the breakdown process. Wait until spring to plant as this will allow the bed enough time to decompose over the winter. As the organic matter disintegrates, it will give rise to beneficial microbes, making the soil rich with nutrients.

*Additional Tip

Once you've harvested your crops, be sure to put away the bed for winter. Toss leftover material from your crops on the bed, turn the soil, and plant a cover crop like crimson clover.

Come next spring, the bed will have shrunk in size. All you need to do now is to fill it up with more layers, add a six-inch soil layer, and start planting. A sprinkle of organic fertilizer like fish emulsion or blood meal will give your plants a jump start. Make sure to water deeply.

DIY Straw Bale Bed

Strawbale beds are fairly easy to make. Let's look at the supplies and equipment needed to construct them.

Equipment Required

- Hand trowel

Supplies

- Newspaper or cardboard
- Bales of straw wrapped with baling twine
- High nitrogen fertilizer (pelletized chicken manure/blood or bone meal)
- Compost
- Star pickets/sturdy stakes and wire for a trellis (Optional)

**Note: Avoid bales made from oats, wheat, or other grains as these could sprout and give the bales a shaggy appearance. Go for lucerne or pea straw instead.

Step 1: Water

Pick a sunny spot in your garden and arrange the straw bales, making sure the cut end faces up. This way, each individual straw absorbs more water. Water them thoroughly with a garden hose, drenching them until the excess runs out. Repeat the process for three days.

The process of conditioning the bales for planting is called "seasoning." It involves watering and adding fertilizer to encourage decomposition. This step not only helps create a soilless medium but also heats up the bales, increasing the rate of decomposition.

Step 2: Add fertilizer

Add two to three cups of nitrogen-rich fertilizer to each bale, making sure to spread it evenly across the surface. Water when you're done to ensure even distribution throughout the bales.

Step 3: Cover

Use plastic sheets or tarp to cover the bales and speed up the seasoning process. If you choose to skip this step, make sure to water the bales more frequently to prevent them from drying. Let them rest for a week before watering and adding fertilizer again. Leave them for another week.

Step 4: Begin planting

After about ten days, you'll notice the temperature of the bales cooling down. Now you can begin planting. Take your trowel and make holes in the bale. Add a variety of plants such as herbs and vegetables. In the center of each bale, plant root crops like beets, potatoes, onions, or carrots.

Step 5: Water regularly

A good irrigation system comes in handy at this stage. Water the bales daily or every two days to prevent them from drying out.

Step 6: Harvest

At the end of the season, after you've harvested a good number of veggies, you'll be left with a nice pile of rich compost to sprinkle around your garden!

DIY Herb Spirals

Herb spirals are the darlings of the gardening world. They're multifunctional, mimicking Mother Nature and building the perfect microclimates for plants. Let's look at the materials required to build one.

Equipment Required

- Sod cutter
- Shovel
- Wheelbarrow

Supplies

- Soil
- Compost
- Corrugated drain pipe (2" wide and 6 ft long)
- Thick cardboard

Step 1: Choose a location for your herb spiral

Pick a flat, sunny spot near the kitchen. You'll most likely use herbs daily while cooking and it'll help having them nearby. The spiral will be almost 5 feet in diameter, so make sure there's enough space.

Step 2: Prepare the area

Time to prepare the site by getting rid of sods or weeds growing in the area. Start by making a circle that's 7 feet in diameter to make room for the mulch barrier that'll go around the spiral.

Step 3: Add weed suppressant and cardboard

Apply weed suppressant on the area and start layering it with cardboard. This will suppress weed growth.

Step 4: Start digging

Grab a shovel and dig a shallow ditch around the area where you'll be building the spiral. This will help protect the first layers of stone. Remember to dig around the circumference of the herb spiral and not outside the mulch barrier.

Step 5: Install an irrigation system

Though this step is optional, I highly recommend it. You'll need to place a 3-foot-tall stake in the center of your spiral. Fasten a corrugated pipe with the stake with some jute twine. The top end of the pipe will poke out of the center of your herb spiral. The other end should reach out of the edge of the spiral, directed toward a pressurized water source.

Step 6: Start building by adding soil

Start by building the outer ring first. The center of the spiral will be the highest, giving it a mound-like appearance. If you're living in the Northern Hemisphere, the highest part or center of the spiral should point west and the structure should be counterclockwise. The lowest part of the spiral should face north.

Begin filling the structure with soil. Plant roots will quickly reach the bottom soil on the outer ring. This won't be the case in the center because of its height, so, if you're looking to cut expenses, you can fill the bottom of the center with poor-quality soil, such as loam and clay. Fill the rest of the ring with dark, compost-rich soil to give your plants a boost of nutrients.

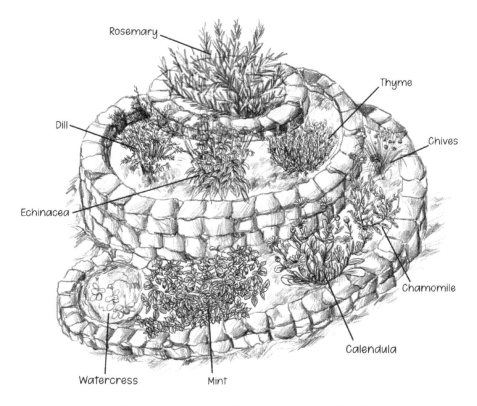

Figure 9: A beautifully constructed herb spiral.

Step 7: Stack up the rocks

Line up the rocks on the outline of the spiral. The structure should be around 3 feet tall. Once you've placed large rocks on the outer ring, start building the walls of the inner rings with medium-sized rocks, stacking them high to create the second and third layers of the spiral.

You can put some rocks in the middle of the walls to decrease the amount of soil required to fill up the spiral and enhance drainage. You can also apply a thin layer of "green manure" under the soil so it acts as compost later.

Step 8: Water

Hose everything down, watering the soil thoroughly and allowing it to settle.

Step 9: Create a mulch barrier

One downside of cutting the grass at the very edge of the spiral is that it could encroach into the structure later, hindering the growth of other plants. For this reason, it's best to get rid of all the grass up until the mulch barrier. For the barrier, fill up the ditch around the spiral with wood chips, cardboard, or straw.

DIY Keyhole Bed

Step 1: Prepare the site

Clear the area in your garden to make space for a keyhole bed. Level the ground. Measure and mark a circle using twine.

Step 2: Lay out the bed

Place a stake in the center of the bed. Wrap some twine loosely to the stake, measure 3 feet away from the center and make a knot. Now, push another stake or a screwdriver through the knot and make a circle in the soil. You can use sand to mark the outline of the bed. This will serve as a visual guide, helping you in the building process.

Step 3: Make an access point for the compost basket

Take the same stake and twine and create an 18-inch diameter circle in the center where you'll be placing the composting basket. Alternatively, you can also use an 18-inch pot. Just slip it over the center stake and your composting basket is ready.

Make sure to build an access point for the compost bin. For this, you're going to draw a wedge leading to the center of the bed. Position the keyhole to the north, which tends to be the shadiest side of the bed. Keep the sunnier areas for growing plants.

Step 4: Construct the walls

Create the first layer of the outer wall following the soil markings. Start stacking bricks, stones, and logs to form the sides of the keyhole. You can also use concrete blocks as the notches in them fit together tightly, creating a stable framework. To stabilize the wall even more, you can place rebar stakes through the middle of every other block.

Adjust the height of your bed to suit your comfort. Start lower and add more height later according to your preference. Just remember to build the composting basket before making the outer wall too high. This can be an enclosed circle or a simple gap for you to easily remove compost.

Step 5: Create the composting basket

An 18-inch wide composting baskeT should be surrounded by porous sides to allow the flow of water and nutrients into the bed. I used a hardware cloth cylinder to make mine, held in place with two rebar stakes. You can use chicken-wire thatching or a row of bamboo stakes to create the basket.

Adding a removable block or panel at the bottom will allow you to easily take out the finished compost during each growing season. Another great idea is to use blocks, gravel, or a layer of mulch in the wedge so it doesn't get blocked with mud.

Step 6: Fill up the bed

The taller the walls, the more difficult it is to fill a keyhole bed. To counter this, you can add part of the soil during the construction phase, smooth it out then add the rest when the walls are finished.

Make sure the top 18 inches are packed with great quality soil and compost mixture. You can use low-quality filler material for the bottom. Some gardeners like to fill the bottom of the bed with layers of soil, wood ash, manure, plant matter, and other biodegradable materials. In time, this bottom layer turns into rich compost.

Step 7: Water

Time to bring out the watering can. Drench the soil and the compost basket. The layers of soil should form a slope away from the basket, so water flows down the sides, trickling into the entire bed. Make sure to always water the composting basket, so the water carries the nutrients to the other plants.

Figure 10: Keyhole garden bed.

Step 8: Start planting

The soil in the keyhole heats up rapidly during spring, so you get a headstart to grow cool-weather vegetables such as lettuce, broccoli, and peas. If you want to enhance aesthetics, you can add some petunias or trailing nasturtiums. Install a trellis over the composting basket for pole beans and vining cucumbers.

Step 9: Turn the compost

Occasionally, turn the compost during the growing season. While the compost basket is a great way to recycle kitchen scraps, it requires regular stirring to keep things fresh and prevent bad odors. After each stirring, apply a new layer of soil, leaves, shredded cardboard, or grass clippings on top.

Key Takeaways

Phew! We've finally done all the hard work and our beds are ready! We started the Chapter by looking at the different materials required for raised beds, the ones we should avoid, and some tips for choosing what's right for our backyards. We moved onto step-by-step guides to construct wooden, keyhole, lasagna, hügelkultur, herb spiral, and straw bale raised beds.

Now that our raised beds are ready, let's move onto the second most important component that could make or break our raised garden bed: the soil!

Chapter 4

Soil Health for Strong Plant Growth

The biggest advantage of using raised beds is improved soil structure and drainage. These nifty structures facilitate soil warming earlier in the season, providing gardeners a leg up for spring planting. Moreover, constructing raised beds can elevate the soil to a more comfortable height ensuring easier maintenance.

Whether motivated by aesthetics or practicality, most gardeners are reembracing the time-tested method of raised-bed gardening for growing vegetables, flowers, and shrubs for better soil health.

Importance of Soil Health

The cornerstone of a thriving garden, whether it be a flourishing vegetable patch or a stunning floral arrangement, hinges on one thing and one thing alone: soil. It isn't merely the medium in which plants take root; it's a dynamic ecosystem teeming with life, overflowing with essential nutrients and offering structural support to your plants.

The well-being of your soil is pivotal for numerous reasons. It serves as a vital source of nutrients for your plants, aids in moisture retention, and bolsters plant resilience against pests and diseases. It forms the bedrock of your garden's ecosystem, fostering biodiversity and vigorous plant growth. Prioritizing soil health empowers gardeners to provide their plants with the optimal conditions for flourishing.

Raised beds present superior soil conditions, improved drainage, and aeration compared to traditional in-ground gardens. They also prolong the growing season by warming the soil earlier and, importantly, they are more ergonomic.

Are you aware of the crucial role soil composition plays in the success of raised beds? Compost is pivotal for promoting soil health, yet its excessive application could end up causing more harm than good.

A fertile soil comprises 45% minerals, 5% organic matter, 25% water, and 25% air. These proportions equate to a growing medium of 70% essential minerals from soil and 30% compost, accounting for the presence of water and air in both soil and compost. For raised beds, this translates to a maximum of a 1–2-inch layer of compost blended into a 6-inch layer of soil.

Soil minerals are non-living substances sourced from a parent material, typically a local geological bedrock. They serve as vital nutrient sources for plants, contributing to plant structure, disease resistance, and enhanced flavor and quality of produce.

Organic materials found in soils encompass living organisms such as microbes, bacteria, fungi, insects, and carbon-based materials from compost. They deliver essential nutrients to plants and serve as a primary energy source for plant tissue development.

Products labeled as garden soil, potting soil, and topsoil often consist mostly of organic material. When you set out to buy soil for your raised beds, look for high-quality mineral-based soil from a reputable supplier who can substantiate their product with soil test reports and detailed content information.

Initially, planting in raised beds mostly filled with compost may lead to favorable outcomes due to readily available plant nutrients. However, as compost ages, nutrient release diminishes, requiring additional compost (or fertilizers) to replenish the dwindling nutrient levels.

The continual use of compost, especially manure-based composts, could lead to phosphorus and ammonium build-up. Excess phosphorus impedes iron and zinc absorption by plants, while excess ammonium increases soluble salt levels, potentially harming plant roots and hindering flower and fruit development. Moreover, excess nitrogen and phosphorus leaching into groundwater can contribute to environmental issues like toxic algae blooms.

Compost is not a sustainable source of potassium, as it is easily lost through leaching. During drought conditions, compost can repel water, increasing run-off. Over time, compost loses its structure and volume, forming a dense, non-porous layer that impedes drainage, reduces soil aeration, and fosters disease. Crucially, many essential minerals required for optimal plant health are not present in significant quantities in compost.

This is why you shouldn't rely on compost alone to ensure good plant health. High-quality soil is much more important than any fertilizer or compost you use. So consider conducting a soil test on your raised beds to assess soil quality and use the necessary amendments. Moreover, during the winter, mitigate nutrient leaching and loss by covering your raised beds with leaf mulch or straw instead of compost.

Maintaining Soil Health

Keep in mind that there's no one-size-fits-all approach to maintaining a great raised garden bed. You've got endless options to play with, so let your creativity run wild and build a garden that's as unique as you are.

Once you've got the raised beds sorted, it's time to talk about soil health—the key to a thriving garden. Luckily, it's not that hard to maintain excellent soil in your raised beds.

The first thing you need to do is to watch out for soil compaction. Don't go stomping all over your beds, or you'll squash those poor roots' chances of getting the water and nutrients they need. Keep your beds narrow and mulch the paths to protect your soil.

Next up, drainage. Dig deep beds to prevent waterlogging, especially if you're dealing with soggy soil. Come spring, give your soil a boost with some organic matter. It's like a slow-release energy drink for your plants, plus it helps hold everything together and attracts all the good bugs.

Remember not to leave your soil out in the cold! Use generous servings of mulch and cover crops to keep the soil cozy and protected from the elements. With these simple tips, you'll be well on your way to a summer garden that's the envy of every gardener in the neighborhood.

Soil Preparation

Let's talk about filling up those raised beds of yours to get your plants off to a healthy start. Because, remember, healthy soil equals happy plants.

First things first, the soil is like the lifeblood of your garden, supplying your plants and all those little critters in the soil with water, air, and nutrients. The dream soil is loose, deep, and crumbly, giving the roots room to roam and letting rain zip through without drowning your plants.

Now, when it comes to filling your raised bed, you want to aim for about 25%-50% organic matter. You can measure this by volume or weight with the help of a soil testing lab.

Got your raised bed area all mapped out? Nice. Now, before you start chucking soil around, take a good look at what you've got. If it's a jungle of weeds and turf, you'll want to start by getting a soil sample tested. This'll give you the lowdown on things like soil pH and nutrient levels, so you know exactly what your plants are getting into.

If you're planning to grow veggies, it's crucial to check for lead in your soil. Anything over 400 ppm and you'll want to steer clear of planting veggies there. Once you've got your soil test results, you can add any recommended fertilizers or soil amendments to give your plants a head start.

If you're dealing with a weedy mess, you've got a couple of options. You can smother those suckers with cardboard or newspaper topped with compost, or go for the weed barrier fabric route. Either way, you'll want to wait a couple of months for everything to kick the bucket before you start planting.

Once your bed's nice and weed-free, it's time to decide whether you're going no-till or minimum-till. No-till means planting straight into the compost layer, while minimum-till involves loosening up the soil a bit with a garden fork or spade before adding your compost mix.

Now, if your soil's more like cement than fluffy goodness, don't worry, you're not alone. Start by giving it a good aeration with a garden fork or spade, then mix in a combo of compost and topsoil to give your plants a fighting chance.

Do you have an existing garden? Lucky you! Assuming your soil's in decent shape, a few inches of compost mixed in with the top layer of soil should do the trick.

And if you're working with a raised bed on a hard surface like a driveway, make sure it's at least 8 inches deep for leafy greens and 12-24 inches for heartier veggies. Fill it up with a mix of compost and soilless growing mix, and you're good to go.

Finally, if you're buying topsoil, be sure to do your homework. Check for soil test results and inspect the soil before you buy. You want something dark and crumbly, not sandy or smelling funny.

How to Prepare the Soil

Picture this: it's spring and you're ready for a bountiful harvest. But as the season wears on, your blooming garden takes a turn for the worst. Plants drooping, pests invading – it's like a garden horror story. But fear not, here's one simple trick to nip those mid-summer blues in the bud–start with top-notch soil.

Think of your soil like a newborn baby, craving a nutritious start to life. Quality is key here because your plants are going to be chowing down on this stuff for months to come. I always say, if you want your garden to thrive, you've got to start with a healthy base. Soil health is the name of the game if you want a garden that's bursting with bounty.

So, what's the secret ingredient for making the best-raised bed soil? Well, there are a few options you can work with. The natural route involves layering branches, wood chips, and paper with straw, grass clippings, and compost. It might sound like a mouthful, but trust me, it's worth it. If you've got a few months to spare, that is. But if patience isn't your strong suit (I'm with you there), I've got a tried and true method that'll have your beds up and running in just a few weeks.

First up, get yourself some primo compost. Think of it as the star of the show, the backbone of your soil. You can snag some from a garden store or even make your own if you're feeling ambitious. Compost should make up the bulk of your raised bed soil, with a smidge of garden mix or topsoil thrown in for good measure.

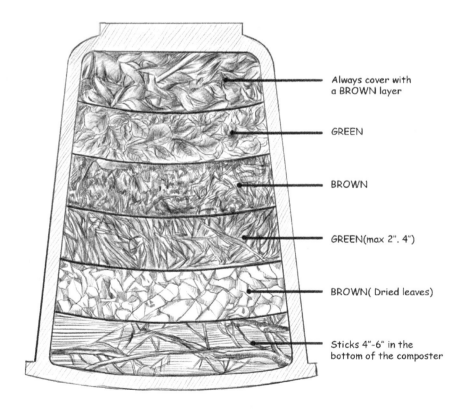

Always cover with a BROWN layer

GREEN

BROWN

GREEN(max 2". 4")

BROWN(Dried leaves)

Sticks 4"-6" in the bottom of the composter

Figure 11: Optimal layers of a compost box.

Next, it's time to jazz things up with some amendments. These come loaded with all sorts of goodies, such as perlite, manure, and gypsum, all designed to give your soil a boost. Mix them into the top layer of compost, and watch your soil come to life.

But wait, there's more! For that extra oomph, sprinkle on some worm castings. These little guys are like gold for your soil, packed with nutrients and beneficial microbes to give your plants a leg up.

Last but not least, give your soil a good drenching. Water it well and let it rest for a week or two, allowing all those ingredients to work their magic and turn your soil into a thriving ecosystem.

The problem with peat moss is that while it has its advantages, it's not exactly a friend to the planet. Peat bogs, where it's harvested from, are crucial for trapping carbon and supporting ecosystems. But over-harvesting has taken its toll, leading to environmental damage and contributing to climate change. So, I've decided to replace peat with more sustainable alternatives like coconut coir or composted bark. Because every bit counts when it comes to protecting our planet.

Key Takeaway

If you want strong plants that can weather stress then start with an excellent soil mix. A strong soil medium enriched with all the essential nutrients is crucial for plant health. The right amount of minerals, organic matter, moisture, and aeration can help plants flourish in the most improbable places. However, getting the soil composition right is just the beginning. Maintaining soil health by using mulch, tilling, providing good drainage, and replenishing nutrients is essential to keep your garden thriving.

Now that we've got the framework ready for a successful raised garden bed, let's move onto the real deal. It's time to choose your crops and start planting! In Chapter 5, we'll discuss the endless possibilities raised beds have to offer for creating diverse garden landscapes.

Chapter 5

Ready, Set, Plant!

Raised-bed gardening offers a simple solution to improve plant health and maximize the productivity of your garden. Better soil structure and good drainage allows the soil in raised beds to warm up faster, enabling early planting during spring. This will give you a head start while the other gardeners are gearing up to plant. And you can forget about those pesky weeds. Your raised bed will take care of those, so you don't have to kneel in the summer heat, yanking them out to get the soil ready for planting.

All you need to do is select plants destined to thrive, and you're all set for a successful harvest.

Plants Suitable for Raised Beds

A wide array of plants including vegetables, herbs, small fruits, flowers, and leafy greens flourish in raised beds. A longer growing season, and well-draining, nutrient-rich soil make raised beds ideal for growing plants such as peppers, carrots, melons, and tomatoes.

While you flip through seed catalogs or wander down the aisles at the gardening center, there are a few points you should keep in mind. Grow what you'd like to eat. Your kitchen garden should cater to your taste palette and nutritional needs. Choose foods that you love to eat, leaving a few rows for trying out new fruit and vegetable varieties.

Consider the length of your growing season while selecting plants you'd like to grow. Choosing crops that will mature during the length of your growing season ensures stress-free gardening. This is where raised beds come into play. If you struggle with a short growing season because you live in a cold climate then raised beds can help you extend it. This will then allow you to grow heat-loving plants with long growing seasons such as hot peppers and melons.

Vegetables

Here are ten vegetables best suited to growing in raised beds:

Bush Beans

Their rapid growth and compact size make them one of the easiest vegetables to grow in raised beds. It only takes 50 to 55 days for most varieties to mature after seeding. It's an excellent warm-season vegetable, planted after the last spring frost. Planting in cold, wet soil may expose the seeds to rot, hindering germination. This makes raised beds the perfect choice for growing them.

Pole Beans

Another bean variety that's an excellent option for home gardeners. Unlike bush beans, these require support and can reach six to nine feet tall. Bean towers, netting, trellises, or bamboo posts can be used to provide the necessary support to these climbing plants.

Sweet and Hot Peppers

Numerous varieties of peppers can be easily grown in home gardens. While sweet peppers tend to have little to no heat, hot peppers range from mild to extremely hot. Both varieties prefer warm, well-draining soil and require adequate moisture. This makes regular watering crucial. Using shredded leaves or straw as mulch can further encourage healthy growth.

Tomatoes

In cooler regions, raised beds can give you a head start on tomatoes. In my old home, I was unable to transplant tomatoes into the ground until mid-June because the soil would be too wet and freezing. With raised beds, I could set them out in late May.

An important thing to keep in mind while growing tomatoes is that they're available in two types: determinate and indeterminate. Determinate varieties, also known as bush tomatoes, can grow up to three to four feet tall. Meanwhile, indeterminate varieties, including vining tomatoes, can reach up to seven or more feet tall. Growing indeterminate tomatoes is slightly more challenging than determinate types as they require sturdy stakes for support. You may also have to tie new growth to the stakes with some string.

Determinate tomatoes are smaller in size, requiring minimal care. Heavy-duty tomato cages can provide the necessary support for growing them. Trailing varieties, such as Terenzo and Tumbling tomatoes, are great for planting along the edge of your raised beds.

Cucumbers

Another warm season vegetable vulnerable to cold temperatures is cucumber. Tender cucumber seeds and seedlings greatly benefit from the early soil warming in raised beds. They come in two main varieties: bush and vining. Bush cucumbers grow only a few feet long, performing well in containers or raised beds. You can use tomato cages to provide them support or simply let them tumble over the sides in your raised bed. Vining cucumbers also do well in raised beds; however, I tend to plant them at the base of A-frame trellises to prevent the more vigorous types from dominating the entire bed.

Carrots

Carrots do well in the deep, loose soil. The same is true for other long-rooted vegetables such as parsnips and daikon radishes. Shallow raised beds, with a depth of 8 inches or less, are better for compact rooted carrot varieties such as baby carrots and Chantenay as well as Parisian kinds which have rounded roots. Raised beds deeper than 12 inches are much better suited to growing long carrot varieties such as Imperator.

Eggplant

A close relative of tomatoes and peppers, this bushy plant flourishes in the summer heat. Before I switched to raised beds, I had to wait at least a few weeks after the last snowfall for the soil to heat up or pre-warm it by using black plastic sheets to cover the ground for 10 to 14 days before planting. Ever since I started using raised beds, I no longer have to worry about pre-warming the soil to set the eggplant transplants off to a good start. The soil heats up early and the water from the spring showers drains away quickly. Tomato cages work best to provide support to the eggplant.

Sweet Potatoes

The tubers require a nice warm growing season. Short season varieties adapt nicely to raised beds. You can plant the "slip ins" in late spring, a week after the last frost date. Soon, you'll have robust little plants filling the garden bed. Cut the leaves and dig out the tubers before the first frost in autumn. You can also munch on the leaves during the summer. Just make sure not to take too many or it may affect tuber development. The tender leaves taste delicious stir fried or steamed.

Leafy Greens

I sow seeds of salad greens like spinach and lettuce as soon as the ground thaws in early spring. These rapidly growing plants love a nutrient-rich soil, making raised beds the best place to grow them. Just sprinkle some compost or manure directly on that area of the bed where you plan to grow them. Sow the seeds or plant the seedlings along the edges so they don't take up too much space. You can also plant fast-growing crops like lettuce and arugula between slower-growing plants such as tomatoes and peppers.

Onions

One of the best options for raised beds, prepare the soil in early spring by adding an inch or two of compost. Plant the onions or seedlings 6 inches apart for big bulbs packed with flavor. The beds should be 4 inches high and 20 inches wide to allow the plants enough room to spread out and attain maximum growth. Water regularly and add food-grade fertilizer rich in nitrogen, phosphorus, alfalfa meal, and potassium each month.

Fruits

We've covered some of the best vegetables to grow in your raised beds. Now let's look at some of the fruits you can try.

Melons

Honeydew, watermelons, muskmelons are the crown jewels of home gardens in the summer. As a novice gardener, whenever I tried growing melons, I ended up with tiny, bland-tasting fruits after late autumn frosts killed most of the vines. I now start harvesting muskmelons in mid-summer, with fresh fruits coming in for at least the next two months. By late summer, my kitchen is packed full with dozens of watermelons and cantaloupes. And, no, I haven't moved south to warmer climates. It's planting in raised beds that made all the difference.

There are several reasons why melons respond so well to raised beds. During spring time, the warmed up soil encourages the tiny seedlings to sprout forth. As a result, these tiny plants begin flowering more quickly. Moreover, the loose, non-compacted soil ensures healthy root growth. Since raised beds have good drainage, the soil doesn't become waterlogged due to spring time rain, making it perfect for growing melons. While melon vines can take up a lot of room, planting them on the sides of the beds or training them up A-frame trellis can help maximize space.

Raspberries

Low-maintenance and easy to grow, they grow well in most soils. However, in raised beds it's easier to cover these brightly colored fruits, protecting them from birds, garden pests, snails and bugs.

Strawberries

Growing strawberries is as simple as growing raspberries. Both berries, perfect for summer fruit salads, can be grown together to keep them contained. Make sure to prepare the soil by mixing it with organic matter or compost before planting. Water and keep a close eye on them as they grow to avoid overcrowding. Raised beds also help keep the weeds at bay, which are a problem with strawberry plants.

Honey Berries

A rather obscure fruit, they're delicious when eaten raw or put in jams or jellies. Their sweetness is similar to blueberries, only they're much larger in size and juicier. You'll need two of them to facilitate fertilization. You may even need to pollinate by hand to keep them fruiting each year, but the payoff makes it worth the effort.

Blackberries

Tired of foraging blackberries each year? Grow them in your raised bed! Usually their rapid growth is cause for concern, but the beds help restrict their growth so they don't end up sprawling across your entire yard.

Currants

Red and black currants can easily adapt to growing in raised beds. While the red variety prefers partial shade, black currants thrive under the full sun. Monitor weather forecasts when you plant as currants don't do so well in harsh conditions such as frigid winters and sweltering summers. Expect a quick harvest. Depending on your location, you might get your first crop within four to six months of planting!

Herbs

Here are some herbs perfect for your raised garden beds:

Cilantro

Cilantro reaps the benefits of improved drainage and loose soil in raised beds. The resulting plant is much healthier, vibrant and resilient against pests. If you plan to grow cilantro from seeds, make sure to select varieties such as Santo, Marino, and Leisure, which tend to be resistant to bolt. Choose a spot that gets the morning sun and rests in shade during noon. You can also plant taller plants next to the cilantro to shield it from the harsh afternoon sunlight.

Basil

Basil roots despise the cold, wet soil. Raised beds not only create the ideal conditions for growing basil, they also protect it from snails and slugs. Just pick a sunny spot, avoid watering in the morning and splashing the leaves with water to prevent powdery mildew.

Rosemary

While it can be planted in spring, summer or autumn, it's best to plant in spring for a year end harvest. Rosemary loves to soak up the sun, so pick a nice bright spot and plant along the wall of the bed. Herbs that grow well with it in herb spirals include sage, oregano, marjoram, lavender, and thyme. Rosemary's ability to deter pests makes it ideal for vegetables such as cabbages, brussels sprouts, shallots, carrots, and beans.

Thyme

Thyme is an excellent addition to any garden. Its flowers draw pollinators like bees while warding off pests like aphids from attacking your vegetables. Plant this amazing herb next to tomatoes and you won't have to worry about tomato hornworms ravaging your crops.

Mint

An excellent choice for novice gardeners, they're easy to grow and require minimal care. In the ground, it may spread rapidly through the garden; however, raised beds help keep its growth in check, preventing unwanted invasion.

Flowers

Some flowers you can have blooming in your raised beds include the following.

Nasturtium

It not only adds to your garden's aesthetic appeal, the leaves and petals are entirely edible, making it an excellent addition to your salads. It needs plenty of sunlight to grow so choose a sunny area. Sprinkle the flowers on your salad, use the leaves as mini wraps or use them to make pesto!

Marigold

Well-draining, high-quality soil and full sun are a must for growing these vibrant, annual flowers. African and French marigolds are the most commonly grown varieties. African marigolds, with their large flower heads (almost 5 inches across), grow up to 10 to 36 inches tall. In contrast, French marigolds tend to be smaller in size and more bushy with the height of 6 to 8 inches and flower heads up to 2 inches across. This makes them best for planting among much taller plants to attract pollinators.

Zinnia

They can be easily grown from seeds, blooming from early summer until the first frost. Resistant to extreme conditions and neglect, these resilient flowers are not only edible but excellent for attracting pollinators to your garden. Toss the blooms into your salad, use as garnish or arrange them on the side of your charcuterie board. But if you're not in the mood to eat them, you can always leave them as is on the plant to draw a string of pollinators ranging from butterflies to bees.

Direct Planting vs. Transplanting

Don't be surprised by the strong opinions some gardeners hold for different planting methods. There isn't a universally agreed upon technique that works for every plant, so you're bound to come across some contrasting viewpoints. Some may swear by transplanting seedlings, while others consider sowing seeds directly into the soil the best way to go about planting.

With so many conflicting opinions, it's understandable to feel confused. So let's look at both methods in detail and answer the million dollar question: does it even matter which method you choose?

Transplanting

The difference between the two techniques boils down to quite simply the location where the seeds are planted. In transplanting the seeds are initially grown in one location then relocated into the garden. You have the option to either grow your own seedlings indoors or buy them from the nursery.

You have to spend extra time and energy to start the seeds indoors as well as buy supplies such as a grow light, light stand and heat mat. However, transplanting is a very satisfying process, making the effort worthwhile. With minimal soil prep, you can have the entire garden bursting with green in no time rather than waiting for the first stems to sprout from the ground. Buying starter plants might prove more expensive, but they give you an edge over buying seeds and transplanting. as well as direct sowing, by fruiting much quickly.

Direct Sowing

You can skip growing the seeds indoors and plant them directly into the soil outside. In this method, there's no need to relocate the plants when they're older. Where you plant the seed is where it will stay and grow. It's a much simpler process compared to transplanting, eliminating the hassle of starting seeds early and worrying about supplies like grow lights and heat mats.

However, there's a catch. Whether the seeds sprout forth depends largely on the weather. This may not be much of a problem during summer, but come spring and winter, growing plants can get tricky. Raised beds can help extend optimal conditions to an extent, but in the case of an extended winter or an extremely rainy spring, you may have to put planting on hold.

What Should You Choose?

As gardeners, we want to choose methods that guarantee success. To do so, we must pay attention to the seeds we have to work with. Tough seeds with thick seed coats fare better when sowed directly into the soil. These include beans, peas, corn, cantaloupe, pumpkin, and squash.

Another great candidate for direct sowing are plants with large seeds. They're much easier to space out, so you don't have to worry about planting them too close together. This is a problem for small seeds, which can be notoriously difficult to separate. If you're not careful, you'll end up planting them too close and have to deal with thinning them out later.

Small seeds are usually vulnerable to low temperatures, making transplanting the best way forward. Start them indoors in soft soil mixtures and transfer the seedlings outdoors when they develop true leaves. Plants with fragile seeds like tomatoes and peppers are also better off being transplanted. However, tiny seeds of leafy greens surprisingly perform well when directly sowed into the soil during winter.

Plants such as lettuce, kale, or spinach can be scattered over the soil and raked in when the weather is cool but not freezing. Brussels sprouts, cabbage, and lettuce can be started indoors or you can buy pelleted seeds, which makes handling small seeds more manageable.

Spacing the Right Way

The success of your raised garden bed hinges on good spacing. While planting, you want to avoid making the bed too crowded or the plants too spread out. New gardeners are usually unable to anticipate the plant's size once they mature and end up overcrowding the plants instead.

There are many downsides of overcrowding including poor air circulation, which can lead to the spread of diseases. Growing in close vicinity to each other, the plant's roots begin competing for food, depriving some plants of the necessary nutrients.

Planting too far apart also presents its own set of problems. The empty spaces give way to weed growth. With fewer shady areas, smaller plants are more exposed to the sun. Moreover, it can hamper cross-pollination.

To get the spacing right, just flip over the seed packet. Here you'll find the size of the mature plant and the necessary spacing requirement.

This is particularly useful for row spacing. Other than that you learn through the tedious process of trial and error.

Over the years I've re-adjusted plant spacing multiple times to find what works best for the climate I live in and the varieties I grow. Table 1 lists the ideal distance between the rows of seeds in your raised bed for different plants.

Table 1: Spacing Requirements of Different Vegetables

Plant	Spacing
Arugula	4 inches
Asparagus	14 inches
Beets	6 inches
Broccoli	18 inches
Brussels Sprouts	18 inches
Cabbage	18 inches (small variety)
Carrot	3 - 4 inches
Celery	10 inches
Collards	12 inches
Cauliflower	18 - 24 inches
Corn	12 inches
Cucumbers	6 inches
Eggplants	24 inches
Garlic	6 inches
Kale	12 - 18 inches
Leeks	8 inches

Lettuce	10 inches
Okra	18 inches
Onion	6 - 8 inches
Parsnip	6 inches
Peas	3 inches
Peppers	18 inches
Pole Beans	4 inches
Potatoes	12 inches (18 inches to 2 feet between rows)
Radishes	4 - 8 inches
Sweet Potatoes	12 inches (18 inches between rows)
Tomatoes	24 - 36 inches
Turnips	4 - 8 inches
Winter Squash/Pumpkins	9 feet or more in all directions (adjust according to variety)
Zucchini/Summer squash	4 feet

Consider the space a particular plant will take up on maturing and plan your raised bed accordingly. The last thing you want is a single pumpkin sprawling over the entire bed or tightly packed salad greens leaving no room for other plants. Keep in mind that climbing vegetables, like pole beans and indeterminate tomatoes, can be trained upward, freeing up space underneath.

When direct sowing, planting the seeds in rows usually yields the best results. Just use your finger to evenly carve rows in the soil and sprinkle one seed packet at a time. Try not to clump them together or densely pack them in one spot. Add a layer of soil on the seeds and pat them down. Make sure to label the plant's name and place it at the end of the row. Repeat the same process for all the seeds.

For carrots and spring onions, sprinkle the seeds sparingly to save yourself the trouble of thinning them out later. You can also place large seeds around the edge and some in the center, if there's space. Remember to water the newly planted seeds generously after sowing and cover the beds with poly bags until the first leaves sprout.

Make sure to rotate the crops year after year, so you're not growing the same plants in the same spot. This will make them more resistant against pests while replenishing lost nutrients in the soil. Moreover, it will give you an idea about spacing, giving you the freedom to experiment with new patterns and combinations the following year.

Companion Planting

Some plants just get along well together while others can't stand each other. Companion planting involves taking advantage of plant friendships to create mutually beneficial pairings for optimal results. Through different combinations of plants, you can impart various characteristics to your garden bed such as repelling pests, creating shade, and fixing soil nutrients. Table 2 lists some beneficial alliances between plants. You can customize the plants you want to grow together based on this list, trying out different combinations for your plants.

Table 2: Best Pairs for Companion Planting

Plants	Best Paired With
Beets	Brassicas, garlic, lettuce, bush beans, onions
Broccoli	Oregano, beets, celery, chamomile, potatoes, and lettuce
Cabbage	Garlic, nasturtium, sage
Carrots	Leeks, peas, onions, rosemary, chives, sage, radishes (Avoid dill, coriander, and celery)
Cucumbers	Beans, dill, lettuce, nasturtiums, radish, oregano
Kale	Onion
Lettuce	Chives, onions, peas, radishes
Onions	Cabbage, kale, lettuce, carrots, strawberry, tomatoes, beets, chard
Tomatoes	Calendula, garlic, onion, thyme, nasturtium, parsley
Peas	Mint, carrots, chives, alyssum, lettuce, turnip, spinach, radish (Avoid onions)
Peppers	Basil, onions, oregano, marjoram
Potatoes	Beans, horseradish, catmint, oregano, garlic
Spinach	Rosemary, cilantro, oregano
Winter squash / zucchini / pumpkin	Oregano, buckwheat, nasturtium, calendula

Plants You Should Not Grow Next to Eachother

While most plants are harmless when grown in close proximity, there are some that shouldn't be paired together. For example, tomatoes and potatoes tend to compete for the same resources. Similarly, carrots, dill and celery compete with each other and other members of the carrot family. Members of the onion family, such as onion, leeks, shallots and garlic, are best kept away from peas as they can stunt their growth.

Furthermore, bear in mind that growing the same plant in a single raised garden bed is akin to throwing a feast for all the pests. The same principle applies when you grow a lot of vegetables from the same family together in one spot. It's a surefire way to draw large populations of the same pests, making it difficult to eliminate them later. Mixing up the plants with different varieties makes them resilient against a number of problems and keeps the pests at bay.

Key Takeaways

We started off this chapter by looking at the plants best suited for raised beds. These include a wide variety of fruits, vegetables, flowers, and herbs. We discussed two different planting methods: direct sowing and transplanting, and how to decide between the two. Spacing the plants in your raised bed might seem uncomplicated, but can be rather tricky. We looked at the spacing requirements of different plants, so you don't end up overcrowding your raised bed.

Companion planting is an ingenious technique to make the most of limited spaces while reaping the benefits various plants have to offer. We looked at many mutually beneficial combinations and some that we should avoid. The next chapter contains planting guides to give us an idea about what to plant and when to plant it.

Chapter 6

Planting Guides

A simple trick to make the most of your raised bed is to group together plants with the same needs. Pair a moisture-loving tomato with an agave that thrives in dry soil and you'll find yourself in a real fix. Despite your best efforts, one of the two is destined to suffer. Small mistakes like these may seem inconsequential at first, but can cost a lot in terms of your time and money. In this chapter, you'll find a comprehensive garden plan so you know exactly what to grow and when.

The Ultimate Garden Plan

From the dimensions of the raised beds to the plants you'll grow, you've got everything figured out. Still, things end up going south and you're left scratching your head. Wouldn't it be great if someone just handed you a set of guidelines, so you weren't blindsided by problems? I sure hope I had it when I started out. Lucky for you that you got your hands on this book because you're about to get just what you're looking for.

I'll share my tried-and-tested planting guides to keep your gardening journey firmly on track and take care of any curve balls heading your way. In this section, we'll look at annual gardening plans for growing vegetables, fruits, and herbs. You'll learn exactly when to plant, sow, and harvest. But before we discuss all that, let's recap some important tips to ensure successful gardening:

Square Foot Gardening Method

The trick to achieve an excellent raised garden bed is to get spacing right. Following the square foot gardening principle allows you to maximize space utilization, so not an inch of your raised bed goes to waste. The technique provides a visual aid to get spacing right. In a 4 by 4 square raised bed, draw a grid of sixteen 1 foot squares. Place a different plant in each square. Keeping the plant's mature size in mind, the total number of plants in the bed can vary from 4 to 16.

Pay Attention to the Roots

While planting, position plants with shallow root systems along the edges, leaving the center for deep-rooted plants to prevent unnecessary competition for nutrients. Most garden beds are 17 inches to 32 inches deep, making them perfect for a wide variety of vegetables, even those with deep root systems.

Plants with 12 to 18 inch roots include garlic, chives, onions, brussels sprouts, spinach, corn, cabbage, radishes, and strawberries. Crops with root systems ranging between 18 to 24 inches in depth include peas, beans, squash, cantaloupes, eggplants, beets, carrots, turnips, and potatoes. Finally, plants with root systems of 24 to 36 inch deep include asparagus, parsnips, rhubarb, artichokes, sweet potatoes, pumpkins, and watermelons.

Succession Planting for the Win

Extend the growing seasons and enjoy an uninterrupted supply of fruits and vegetables through succession planting. Prepare a list of the plants you want to grow and find out their growing seasons. The next step is to create a plan so the second crop replaces the first soon after harvest.

This is what a common succession pattern looks like: Planting cool season crops in early spring, followed by warm season crops in late spring or early summer then growing another cool season crop in mid to late summer. The temperature requirements for warm season plants range between 70 to 85°F (21-29°C). They need protection if the temperature dips below 50°F (10°C). As for cool season plants, the average temperature of the air and soil should hover between 60 to 75°F (15-24°C). Anything above 80°F (27°C) can damage these cool loving plants.

Vertical Gardening

Free up space in your garden beds by training your vining vegetables on trellises and stakes. Maximize vertical spaces so you have more room to grow in your raised beds. Training plants upward increases their access to sunlight while improving air circulation and making pest detection easy.

Now that we know what it takes to reap a successful harvest, let's look at a simple gardening plan for five beds. Here's what you can grow in each of them during spring and summer months:

Raised Bed 1

Bring out the peas, cucumbers, and marigolds. Set up a few stakes for the peas and add a vertical trellis for cucumbers. We learned in the previous chapter how cucumbers and peas are the best pals when grown together. Well, come March or April, it's time to put the theory to test. Pair them with some marigolds and you've taken care of most pest problems while attracting loads of beneficial pollinators to your garden.

Raised Bed 2

The second bed is for delicious greens like kale, spinach and lettuce along with a few radishes, beets, and onions. I like to think of this as my salad bar. The kale I harvest is more than sufficient and I often end up blanching and freezing it for soups and smoothies that I'll be enjoying in the winter. You can also toss beets in the mix, if you like. They grow well with leafy greens not just in the ground but also in the salad bowl.

Raised Bed 3

This is where you plant your cilantro, basil, dill, tarragon, and strawberry. Chances are you might end up with more than you need with this winning combination. Turn the excess basil, kale, and spinach into pesto and freeze. I like to spread the blended pesto onto parchment paper in burger patty-sized portions before placing them in the freezer. After freezing, just lift the patties off the paper and transfer them to freezer bags and you're all set for the entire year!

Raised Bed 4

Here's where you plant your carrots, broccoli, green beans, nasturtiums, cabbage, and green onions. Plant the carrots, broccoli, and green onions on one side and the rest on the other for extra protection from pests.

Raised Bed 5

There's no reason to leave out pretty ornamental flowers from your garden design. The fifth bed is a burst of color with cherry tomatoes, jalapeno peppers, bell peppers, parsley, and marigolds in full bloom. This garden bed is not only a visual treat but crucial for drawing pollinators and other beneficial insects, which in turn take care of the pests.

In my home, the cherry tomatoes and peppers are all used up. As for the parsley, I freeze the excess in a bag. The same goes for other herbs I want to store. Just place them in a Ziploc bag, roll it up, and toss them in your freezer. Make sure to label them, so you don't end up adding parsley or basil to your mint lemonade!

By now, you may have an idea about what to grow in your raised beds. To make things easier, let's round up all the vegetables, fruits, and herbs you can grow during the spring and summer season in a neat little timeline. Keep in mind that this gardening plan is based on Zone 8 recommendations and will work best for people in the Pacific Northwest. However, it can give you a general idea about which plants to pair together and when to grow them.

January
- Sketch out your garden.
- Order seeds.
- Make a list of the seedlings.

February
- Finish seed orders.
- Read instructions on the packet and make a chart of the dates to start them.
- Note the germination rate of each plant; how long it takes for the first leaves to emerge from the seeds.
- Decide on the planting day for each plant.
- Stock up on growing mix and seed trays.
- Buy the necessary tools.

Plants to Grow:
- Plant bare root perennial vegetables outside such as artichokes, rhubarb, horseradish, and asparagus.
- Indoors you can start seeds for cool-season vegetables such as cabbage, spinach, lettuce, onions, broccoli, and kale.

March
- Do a soil test. Measure the pH and nutrient content.
- Make adjustments to the soil by adding conditioners such as peat moss, compost and coir to improve texture, organic compost or manure and fertilizer to enhance nutrient content.

Plants to Grow:
- Indoors you can start seeds for warm-season plants like peppers, eggplant, pumpkin, tomatoes, snap beans, sweet beans, sweet corn and squash.
- Check the soil temperature with a thermometer. If it's above 40F then start planting seeds of cool-season vegetables such as kale, spinach, lettuce, cabbage, broccoli, beets, carrots, radish, cilantro and onions.
- Plant peas at the end of the month.

April

- Keep row covers on hand to protect your plants in case of a nighttime cold snap.
- Check soil temperature. If it's 60°F or more, go ahead and plant your warm season crops.
- Buy transplants, if you don't want to opt for started seeds, for early-season plants such as spinach, leeks, onions, radishes, beets, carrots, brussels sprouts, spinach, and peas.

Plants to Grow:

- You can plant marigolds outside and start the following plants indoors: basil, parsley, peppers, tomatoes, Brussels sprouts, green beans and onions.
- Set out the transplants, preferably on an overcast day to minimize shock, and water. Add a two to three inch layer of mulch to suppress weeds and increase water retention.
- Plant seeds outside in succession, planting some every few weeks for a continuous harvest.

May

- Keep an eye on soil temperature. If it's consistently above 70°F, get ready to plant heat loving plants such as peppers and tomatoes.
- Make sure you have a good irrigation system involved or a handy watering can because your plants will need a consistent moisture level.
- Keep an eye on cool-season crops like asparagus, spring greens, and peas, which will be nearing harvest.
- Look out for insect damage (holes or pits on leaves) to detect pest problems.

Plants to Grow:
- Plant early-season plants such as squash, eggplant, melons, tomatoes, peppers, sweet corn, potatoes, herbs and cucumbers.
- You can sow beets, radishes, and carrots.

June

- This month is all about. maintenance and harvest.
- Thin out the seedlings of plants directly sown earlier.
- Stake the plants that require support.

- Add organic compost and root out the weeds.
- Continue harvesting greens, beans, peas, and herbs.
- Stop harvesting rhubarb and asparagus so you can have a good crop next year.

Plants to Grow:
- Sow all the warm-season vegetables you want to grow such as swiss chard, summer squash, radish, okra and corn.

July
- Harvest cucumbers, cauliflower, beans, carrots, and other cold-season vegetables.
- Enrich soil with compost before planting seedlings or direct sowing seeds.
- Prune any suckers (growth between the main stem and leaf) you find on your tomato plants.
- Continue staking tomatoes and other plants that require support.

Plants to Grow:
- You can sow determinate tomatoes, basil, squash, beans, and sunflowers.

August
- Take note of your successes and failures so you don't repeat them next season.
- Keep a check on soil moisture level and watch out for insects and disease.
- Discard decaying fruits and fallen leaves.
- Keep harvesting, freezing, drying, and storing for use over winter.

Plants to Grow:
- You can continue planting cool season crops like kale, brussels sprouts, cauliflower, cabbage, chives, spinach, lettuce, turnips, radishes, peas, parsnips, onions, celery, and Swiss chard.

September
- Use covers or sheets to protect tender plants like tomatoes.
- Prepare the beds for spring or build more raised beds.
- Plant cool-season vegetables for winter harvest.

- Clear dead plants and discard rotten fruit.
- Reapply mulch.

October
- Use row covers to protect winter crops and new seedlings.
- Collect dead leaves for the compost pile.
- Dismantle and remove the stakes and cages used for plant support, storing them for next year.
- Harvest the potatoes and store in a dark place with low humidity.
- Harvest fall crops like leeks, chard, cabbage, and beets.

November
- Begin planning for January and order seed catalogs.
- Water cool-season plants if there isn't sufficient rainfall.
- Apply water-soluble organic fertilizer to your vegetable plants.
- Cut down asparagus plants, if they've turned yellow or brown, and spread manure or organic compost on the bed.
- Pick greens and other cool-season vegetables that continue to ripen.

December
- Keep harvesting if you planted a winter garden, watering and weeding as required.

January
- Force rhubarb plants to give rise to fresh pink shoots. Use an upturned container to keep the plants in the dark to encourage sweeter and more tender stems.
- This is a good time to prune established trees and vines such as apples, grapes, gooseberries, currants, and grapes.
- Plant apples, blackcurrants, blueberries, cherries, figs, pears, plums, raspberries, red and white currents.

February
- Stock up on strawberry plugs and bare-rooted plants.
- Prune autumn raspberries, apples, currants, pears, and gooseberries.
- Continue planting the fruits listed above.
- Start planting grapes.
- Start alpine strawberries indoors.

March
- Protect pear and plum flowers from frost with fleece covers.
- Prune plums and cherries.
- Harvest rhubarbs

- Continue planting blackberries, raspberries, and other berry plants.
- Continue sowing alpine strawberries indoors.
- Start cape gooseberries indoors.

April
- Use fleece covers to protect apple, blackcurrant , pear, and plum blooms.
- Look out for signs of pests.
- Prune apricots, cherries, figs, nectarines, peaches, and plums.
- You can start planting strawberries outside, Make sure to protect them from frost with row covers.
- Continue growing alpine strawberries indoors.
- Transplant gooseberries outdoors.
- Plant cranberries.
- Start melons indoors.

May

- Continue pruning apricots, nectarines, peaches, and plums.
- Use straw or strawberry mats to protect the strawberry seedlings from soil splashes and rot.
- Begin hardening off alpine strawberries for planting outside in mid-May.
- Protect tender young fruits from birds using nets or pest covers, in late summer, once fruiting has finished.
- Weed out strawberry beds and the area around fruit trees and bushes.
- Tie new growth to support structures on trained apple, pear, or other fruit trees.
- Pick gooseberries and early strawberries.
- Continue transplanting cape gooseberries. You can also begin planting them outside.
- Continue planting gooseberries, melons, summer and perpetual strawberries.

June

- Remove the strawberry runners that have finished producing and peg down the ones you want to keep.
- Weed out strawberry beds, around the fruit tree and bushes.
- Thin fruit trees for larger harvests.
- Secure new growth on grape vines, blackberries, hybrid berries, and raspberries.
- Prune adult plum trees (more than 4 years old) until July.
- Prune red and white currants, and gooseberries.
- Pick black, red, and white currants, summer raspberries, and strawberries.

July

- Plan how to water, care, and harvest your plants over the summer. You may need to organize a rota for watering and picking the fruits.
- Net pears and grapes to protect them from birds and wasps.
- Keep securing young growth In hybrid berries, raspberries, blackberries, and grapes.
- Prune gooseberries and pears.
- Harvest blueberries, plums, gooseberries, raspberries and strawberries.

- Clean up strawberry plants. Cut away and pot up any runners you want to keep or transfer them to a new bed.

August
- Prune trained pears.
- Harvest blueberries, early apples, plums, early pears, summer raspberries and blackberries.

September
- Prune apples.
- Chop old canes on summer raspberries, blackberries, and hybrid berries after all the fruit is picked. Secure any new growth.
- Winter prune gooseberries and currants.
- Harvest blackberries, mid-season apples, grapes, blueberries, early pears, mid-season plums, autumn raspberries and hybrid berries.
- Plant strawberries and raspberries outside for a small harvest next summer.

October
- Plan the fruit plants you'll grow next year and order fruit trees and bushes.
- Clean the raised bed where the new fruit trees will be planted, remove weeds and add compost.
- Install stakes and wires where you plan to grow blackberries, raspberries, and hybrid berries.
- Prune gooseberries, hybrid berries, currants, and blackberries.
- Harvest grapes, apples, blackberries, and autumn raspberries.
- Start building raised beds for the next growing season.
- Plant grapes, blackberries, and raspberries.
- Keep planting strawberries. For an early start, you can also plant a few in pots and keep indoors.

Herb	Start Indoor	Plant Outdoor	Days to Maturity
Basil	Anytime	March to August	70 days
Catnip	4 to 8 weeks before the final frost	April to June	75 days
Chives	Anytime	April to May	80 days
Coriander	2 weeks before the final frost	March to August	65 days
Dill	October to April	March to August	60 days
Lavender	Anytime	April to May /August	2 years
Lemongrass	February to March	March to August	75 days
Mint	Anytime	April to May	60 days
Oregano	Anytime	April to May	85 days
Parsley	Anytime	March to August	80 days
Rosemary	Anytime	April to May	85 days
Sage	Anytime	April to May	70 days
Thyme	Anytime	April to May	80 days

Key Takeaways

The planting guides in this chapter provide a roadmap for you to follow as you get started on your gardening journey. The entire process of deciding which plants you should grow and figuring out the best time of the year to grow them can feel a little overwhelming, especially for new gardeners. The planting timelines give you an idea of which tasks you should anticipate and which plants you should grow in different months.

With the mammoth task of planning and organizing our produce out of the way, let's move on to my favorite part: harvesting! In the next chapter, we'll look at different irrigation methods to keep our raised beds hydrated and the various harvesting techniques we can use.

Chapter 7

Growing and Harvesting

There's nothing better than walking through your own garden and admiring the fresh produce. Raised beds give you the freedom to grow what you want with ease, but the innovative design requires a few special considerations. One of these, and arguably the most important one, is irrigation. Figuring out which irrigation system works best for your garden is the cornerstone of good gardening. Without the proper irrigation techniques, your plants may not get sufficient water, giving rise to dehydration and disease.

Irrigation Systems

With the many irrigation systems available these days, you don't have to haul a heavy watering can through your garden day and night to keep your plants hydrated. Let's look at five essential irrigation techniques to keep your raised garden beds flourishing all year long.

Drip Irrigation

If you're searching for a more long-term solution, then drip irrigation could be right for you. The setup involves multiple connecting tubes or hoses with emitters fixed at specific points delivering water directly to the plants' roots. The soil absorbs moisture through drip lines, leaving little room for waste or evaporation. The minimal water wastage makes drip irrigation the ideal choice for raised beds, allowing you to conserve resources while making sure your plants are evenly watered.

You can either purchase drip irrigation kits designed especially for raised gardens or create your own. It involves connecting a timer-controlled valve to a spigot and a network of tubes spreading through the entire garden.

Soaker Hoses

Soaker hoses are long porous tubes that release small amounts of water. They're excellent for raised beds and can be installed along the perimeter of the bed for a consistent water supply. All you need to do is to simply turn on the water flow, sit back and relax. One downside of using soaker hoses is that they can get clogged easily and may sometimes develop cracks, leading to water loss. Moreover, they don't always water plants evenly.

Sprinkler System

Sprinklers are another great option for raised garden beds, as they deliver water quickly to large areas. You can install a sprinkler system on your own, making sure to select the right type of nozzle and laying down the pipes so that water is distributed evenly through your garden beds.

A possible disadvantage of using sprinkler systems is that they may encourage the spread of disease through water droplets. They can also lead to excess water loss by not providing plants with adequate moisture. The water may not penetrate deep into the soil and is lost through evaporation.

Hand Watering

If you've got only a few raised beds to work with, then it makes little sense to opt for elaborate irrigation systems. In such cases, your trusted watering can or hose can get the job done more quickly and efficiently. Choose an adjustable nozzle and you're all set to go! While hand watering is a great option if you're looking to cut costs, it can be somewhat time-consuming. I'd suggest making a one-time investment on a good irrigation system, if you plan to expand your garden.

Tips for Watering Raised Beds

Oftentimes, the difference between a healthy garden and one that's not doing so well comes down to proper watering. A good irrigation system provides a raised garden bed with a consistent and even water supply. It's easy to use and install, requiring minimal maintenance. However, the story doesn't end once you decide on the right irrigation system. You may notice your plants struggling with over or under watering even with the best irrigation systems installed. Here are some tips to make sure this doesn't happen and your plants receive their daily water requirements.

1. Spend time in your garden

Regardless of which method you choose, it's important to keep a close eye while it's operating. Automatic systems give you the comfort of programming the watering schedule, so it can run without supervision. However, being physically present in the garden during watering allows you to detect problems before the health of your plants is compromised. A dead battery, broken timer or a leak can lead to over or under watering. Without proper supervision, you may not find out about these problems until it's too late.

2.   Keep the weather in mind

How much you water and how frequently depends on the weather. When it's dry, windy or scorching hot, you'll have to water your plants more than usual. Similarly, if you live in a city where the summer's particularly hot, you have to water your plants more frequently. During the winter or in places that are cold year round, you may not feel the need to water more than a few times a week. The bottomline is to adjust the quantity and frequency of water based on seasonal changes and weather conditions.

3.   Water according to your plants' needs

Watch for signs of watering stress. Brown leaves with dry edges and curled tips, wilting, leaf shedding and drooping branches signal underwatering. Plants wilting during the afternoon and recovering by evening or the following morning may be going through heat stress. You may have to increase watering in such cases or arrange shade for your plants.

Toughen up your plants by avoiding over watering. This encourages them to develop some level of heat tolerance, promoting healthy growth. Soft, soggy roots with an unpleasant smell are a clear indication of root rot. Scale back on watering and allow the soil to dry out. Overwatering may also cause the leaves to curl, become yellow, and drop.

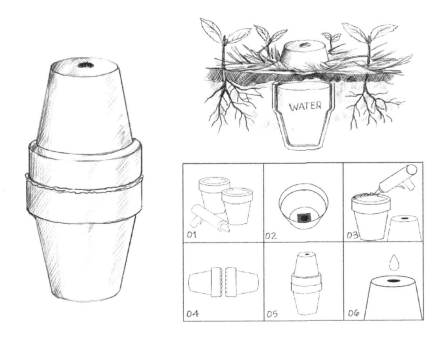

Figure 12: Example of a DIY self-watering terracotta pot.

4.   Water less often, but deeply

Water deeply enough to reach the roots of the plant. If you're unsure you've watered well enough, use a long metal object to check the moisture level of the soil deep in the raised bed. If the soil underneath appears dry, you may have to water a bit more.

Wait until the top two inches of the soil dry out before bringing out the watering can or switching on the sprinklers. Occasionally, water twice as long to drain excess salts from the soil and prevent salt burns.

5.   Start the day by watering your plants

What better way to start the day than by spending some time in your garden? Watering your plants early in the morning provides them the necessary hydration before the afternoon sun heats up the soil. Morning watering sessions may also prevent the spread of waterborne disease and pests.

6.   Be consistent

This is where automatic systems come in handy. You can simply program them to water consistently and evenly. Depending on the weather, simply adjust the watering frequency. When watering manually, make sure to follow a set watering schedule. Inconsistent watering makes the plants vulnerable to pests and diseases, drying out seeds and seedlings and leading to an onslaught of numerous other problems.

Bring In the Harvest!

It's that time of the year we've all been waiting for! Finally, we get to see the fruits of our labor. Harvesting fruits and vegetables from your garden is a rewarding task, if done right. Pick them too soon or too late and you'll be underwhelmed by the taste and texture. Seed packets and plant tags provide valuable information such as the number of days before maturity. However, the ripening process may vary depending on numerous factors such as the weather and soil fertility, making it somewhat difficult to judge when to harvest.

The good news is that fruits and vegetables provide a number of clues to indicate whether they're ready to be picked. Let's look at some harvesting principles to help you decode these clues, so you never go through the disappointment of staring at an unripe tomato or a mushy eggplant that's only good for going in the bin.

Harvesting Principles

To pick, or not to pick! Here are a few principles to give you a general framework of when and how to harvest your garden produce:

1. **Wait for peak flavor and nutrition** - Most vegetables such as peas, turnips, and summer squash achieve their highest nutritional value as well as taste best when they're tender and immature. Other plants such as melons and winter squash must ripen completely while attached to the vine.

2. **Size them up** - The size of your fruit or vegetable is usually a reliable indicator of whether it's ready. Always check the seed packet to get an idea of the size your fruit or vegetable will assume on maturity.

3. **Pick often** - Make a habit of harvesting regularly. Some fruits and vegetables go bad if left on the plants for too long. For example, beans can turn tough from tender in a matter of days. A two-foot-long zucchini club that's ready for harvest today can become overripe in just a day or two. Moreover, frequent harvest also encourages the plants to produce more.

4. **Keep the right tools on hand** - While some crops like peas, kale, and lettuce snap off easily, requiring no fancy tools, others have to be cut off. A sharp pair of shears, knives, or hand pruners can help take care of tougher stems of plants such as cucumbers and eggplants. A garden fork can cut down the time it takes to harvest root crops such as potatoes.

5. **Harvest at the right time** - Timing is key for harvesting crops at their peak flavor. Fruits and vegetables are at their best at the time of maturity. Wait any longer and you'll notice a sharp decline in quality. Early mornings are usually considered the best time to harvest when the fruits are at their juiciest and sweetest. For vegetables, avoid picking leafy greens in the afternoon heat or they might wilt following the harvest.

6. **Show some TLC** - Keep vines properly fastened to support structures so the weight of ripened crops doesn't cause

breakage. Try not to tug or rip while picking, so you don't cause unnecessary damage to the plants, which can serve as an entry point for pests.

7. **Work from the outside in** - Snap off the outer, larger leaves when harvesting leafy greens such as lettuces. Leave the tiny, younger growth in the center untouched.

Guidelines for Harvesting Vegetables

Here are some tips for harvesting different vegetables:

Arugula

Cut or pinch off each leaf individually when they're 2 to 3 inches in length. Young leaves may be more flavorful but older leaves are also edible unless the plant starts to bolt. The leaves taste rather bitter after bolting.

Asparagus

Pinch off the spears when they're 6 to 8 inches in height. Bend each spear until it snaps off or use a sharp knife to cut the stems near the soil surface. Harvest for 4 to 8 weeks until the new growth appears thinner with loose and open tips.

Beans

Pick pole or bush beans when the pods assume the thickness of a pencil, with small, underdeveloped beans inside. At this stage, the pods should snap off with ease. Slender, immature pods are usually not high on flavor. Pods with bulging, oversized beans are overripe and are tougher and lacking flavor.

Beets

Dig the beets when they reach one to two and a half inches in diameter. Large-sized beets may be edible but they're not very flavorful. Although they prefer cool weather, it's best to dig them up before the first hard frost.

Broccoli

Cut off the heads when the buds are tightly packed and dark green, ranging 3 to 6 inches in diameter. Using a sharp knife, cut the stalk at least 6 inches below the head.

Brussels Sprouts

Start harvesting when the sprouts are 1 to 1½ inches, firm and tightly packed. Break the sprout at the base of the stalk. You can twist or use a knife to cut.

Cabbage

Your cabbage is ready when the head is the size of a softball or a little larger. Check if it's firm and cut at the bottom. If left on the plant for too long, the mature head may continue to grow and split open.

Carrots

Dig them up when they're an inch in diameter. They grow right at the soil line so you can easily check the size. If the soil is loose, simply grab the foliage and pull to check the size then use a garden fork for the harvest. Make haste to harvest the spring planted carrots or the summer heat might turn them bitter and fibrous. Fall planted carrots can remain in the beds over winter, provided they're protected with a generous layer of straw.

Cauliflower

Keep a close eye as it reaches maturity, it can go from perfect to inedible in the blink of an eye. The best time to harvest it is just before the curds that make up the head separate or assume a yellow coloring. Simply cut the stem just below the head, leaving a few leaves attached. If you wait too long, the heads will start splitting open and bolt.

Chard

Snip off each leaf, starting from the outside, leaving the middle untouched. You can also cut the plant an inch above the soil.

Cucumber

Take the pickling kind off the vine with pruners or a knife as soon as they're 2 to 6 inches long. For slicing, burpless cucumbers, wait until they're 6 to 8 inches long. Their skin should be glossy and dark green. If they appear dull or yellowish, with blossoms at the end, then they're way past their prime and packed full of seeds.

Eggplants

Cut the eggplants with a pair of sharp pruners or knife. Leave some of the stem attached. The best time to harvest is when they've reached half their estimated mature size. The skin should have a glossy sheen with a uniform color. Overripe eggplants feel soft and appear dull.

Kale

Pick the leaves when they're 6 to 8 inches long. You can either snap them off with your fingers or use a knife. Work your way from the outside in, staring at the bottom of the plant. You can also harvest 2 to 3 inch long baby leaves for the salads.

Leeks

Harvest when they're 1 inch in diameter. Loosen the soil with a garden fork to pull the leeks from the ground.

Lettuce

The heads are ready to be picked if they feel full and firm when pressed, reaching 6 inches in diameter. Use a knife and cut close to the roots.

Muskmelon

They're ready for harvest when the fruit pulls easily from the stem with a gentle tug. If you have to use a lot of force to separate the melon then it's not ready. Other signs of ripeness include a sweet aroma, the fruit should yield slightly when squeezed at the blossom end, and the rind color should change from green to yellow.

Honeydew Melon

It's ripe and ready when the blossom end feels soft and the rind turns completely white or yellow. Cut the fruit from the vine. Unlike muskmelon, it will not separate readily when pulled.

Watermelon

It's ready to be picked when the rind on the underside starts turning cream or yellow colored from greenish white. The rind on top should be dull, not glossy. Cut from the vine, leaving 2 inches of the stem.

Green Onions

Also known as scallions, harvest these when the stalks reach 6 inches tall. Simply grasp the stalks and pull straight up.

Onion

Harvest when the bulbs are 1 to 2 inches in diameter. Two-thirds or more of the top should have dried. Dig them up with a garden fork.

Parsnips

For the best taste, harvest just after the first few frosts. Sugars concentrate in the parsnips at cold temperatures, making them sweeter. You can also leave them in the ground throughout winter under a thick layer of straw or mulch, then harvest in early spring before the top starts growing again. Any later than that and they'll lose their flavor and texture. Loosen the soil with a garden fork then pull them from the ground. Cut the leaves ¼ inches above the root.

Peas

Snip the pods with pruners, and scissors or break with a gentle tug. Make sure to harvest daily because overripe peas signal the vine to stop producing more.

Pick snow peas as soon as they reach a mature size just before the sweet, tiny peas fill the pod. For sugar snap peas, harvest when the peas are plump inside the pods that snap when pulled much like bean pods.

English or shelling peas should be harvested when the tough, stringy pods are still green, plump, and firm. This shows the peas have filled out the pods. You can also do a taste test by popping open one of the pods and tasting the peas inside. They should taste sweet and juicy.

Sweet Peppers

You can pick them whether they're ripe or not, but always make sure to make a sharp cut with a knife or shears. Twisting and pulling will likely damage the plant. Unripe green peppers don't taste as sweet as when they are allowed to fully ripen, changing from green to red, orange, and yellow. The more you pick, the more the plant will produce. If left on the vine to ripen completely, you'll have sweeter but fewer fruits.

Hot Peppers

Just like sweet peppers, you can pick them at any stage by cutting from the stem. Mature, red hot peppers are spicier than the green ones.

Potatoes

Harvest tender new roots right after the plant flowers, approximately six to eight weeks following planting. Upturn the soil with a garden fork, unearthing one or two potatoes to check. If they seem ready, you can leave the rest underground for two weeks for a bigger harvest, even when the plants above die out. This allows them to develop thicker skins. Use a garden fork, pushing it straight down, almost 8 inches from the middle of the plant before angling it inward. Take care not to pierce or bruise the crops. If damaged, use the potatoes right away because they will invariably spoil. Store the rest in a dry, dark place like a cellar.

Radishes

Spring radishes are harvested when they're still quite small, with a diameter of 1 inch. Leave them in the ground too long and they develop a hot, sharp taste and a pithy texture. Harvest them by grabbing the leaves and pulling them out of the ground.

Rhubarb

Harvest established plants in mid-spring when the leaves are fully developed. Yank them up by the stalks, twisting sideways and away from the center. Cutting can cause damage to the crown of the plant, creating an entry point for disease. Keep harvesting until mid-summer until they become stringy. Avoid removing more than two-thirds of each stalk as over-harvesting can cause the plant to lose vigor. Remember that the leaves are not edible due to their oxalic acid content. For this reason, cut the stalk at an inch or two below the leaves.

Spinach

Start harvesting the leaves when they're 3 inches long. Begin picking from the outside. Smaller leaves are more flavorful than large, puckered ones. Moreover, the tender stems are easier to pinch off. Older leaves are usually more fibrous, requiring a sharp pair of scissors or pruners to be snipped off. Harvest until the plant produces flower stalks. This is a sign that the plant has finished growing and is about to bolt, making the leaves taste bitter.

Summer Squash

They taste best when small and tender. They become packed full of seeds, losing flavor when the skin toughens. Cut the fruit from the vine at mid-morning when the dew has dried. Keep a close eye on the fruits because ripened squash can go bad in a day or two.

Winter Squash

Mature fruits assume color completely while the vines dry out and shrivel. The rind is hard and scratch-resistant. Use a few pruning shears to cut the mature squashes from the vine, but leave a few inches of the stem attached to the plant.

Zucchini

They're ready for harvest when they're about 6 to 8 inches long and 1½ to 2 inches in diameter.

Sweet Potatoes

Yellowing leaves are a telltale sign that your sweet potatoes are ready for harvest. Dig them up once they reach mature size (depending on the variety grown) before the first frost. Use pruners to cut the vines then gently lift the roots from the ground with a garden fork.

Tomatoes

Harvest when they've ripened completely but still firm to the touch. They'll separate easily from the plant with a little upward twist. If they don't break easily, use scissors or pruners to cut them near the stems. Harvest unripened tomatoes before hard frosts, allowing them to finish the ripening process at room temperature indoors.

Turnips

Harvest when they reach 2 to 3 inches in diameter. The flavor will be mild and sweet at this point. Pull them from the leaves or use a garden fork to free them from the soil. Make sure to harvest before the ground freezes.

Guidelines for Harvesting Fruits

Whether a particular fruit is ready for harvest or not depends on the fruit variety and your location. Generally, berries such as strawberries and raspberries ripen around the end of June to mid-July (Check Planting Guides for Fruits in Chapter 6). November is best for harvesting avocados while citrus fruits are usually ready by winter. You'll want to pick your mulberries by April while mangoes ripen by fall.

You can check the ripeness by tasting a fruit or two. Its taste, texture, and color will give you an idea of whether it's ready for picking. If the fruit starts falling off the trees, it's a good idea to bring out the harvest basket and start picking. However, this doesn't apply to all fruits such as pears. It's best to look for signs of maturity. Apples are ready when they feel firm and taste sweet and crunchy. Meanwhile, plums should feel tender and juicy.

Quince and medlars may not taste so good if picked early. It's better to leave them on the trees; however, be sure to harvest before the first frost.

Gooseberries can be picked even if they're underripe and turned into jams or left to ripen. Red currants and acid cherries are ripe when swollen, deep colored, and soft to the touch, but they'll always taste sour. Harvest cooking apples when the first fruits begin to drop. They can be harvested even if they taste a little sour. Dessert apples can also be picked when they're slightly underripe.

Handle the fruit with care. Avoid applying too much pressure while you pull to prevent bruising. With minimal finger pressure, hold the fruit in your palm and gently twist until it breaks free. It should come away easily, with a little stalk intact. Peaches, nectarines, and apricots need extra care while harvesting. Hold them in your palm and press near the stalk with your fingertips. The fruit should feel soft in your hand and separate from the stem with ease.

Harvest currants while they're attached to each other and separate later. Use a pair of scissors to cut cherries. As for delicate fruits, like mulberries and goji berries, shake the tree with a sheet of cloth placed underneath. The ripe berries will break free and fall on the cloth.

Key Takeaways

Watering your raised garden bed doesn't have to be a back-breaking task you dread. With the many automatic irrigation systems on hand, you can customize watering sessions according to your plant's needs. While hand watering remains a classic, other techniques such as sprinkler systems, drip irrigation, and soaker hoses can bring some much-needed comfort.

Deciding when to harvest your crops can be confusing. However, there are clues you can look for. Signs of maturity for fruits and vegetables vary. Adapt the right harvesting method for each crop for maximum flavor and quality.

Give yourself a pat on the back because we've almost made it to the finish line. In the next chapter, we'll look at some common problems you may encounter during your gardening journey. From pesky pests to hungry wildlife, you'll learn to tackle each problem head-on. Armed with the strategies outlined in the next chapter, you'll be ready to overcome any obstacle that comes your way and keep your garden thriving.

Chapter 8

Common Garden Problems

As gardeners, we've all been there. You put in your all to make your garden flourish and thrive only to then have a pest move in and ravage your crops. The stems shrivel, the leaves drop and, before you know it, your plant is beyond the point of recovery. Keeping your plants safe can feel like an uphill battle sometimes, but the good news is that raised beds provide better opportunities for handling pest problems. For starters, you have more control on the soil, with the frames acting as a physical barrier to keep out most intruders. Still, you may encounter a few unwanted visitors every now and then, so let's start by familiarizing ourselves with the usual suspects.

Common Garden Pests

Ever noticed tiny holes in your spinach or lettuce while watering them? There's a good chance those are caused by leaf miners, flea beetles, or several tiny pests that feed on tender greens.

Some pests you'll likely find in your garden include

- Slugs

- Aphids

- Squash bugs

- Squash vine borers
- Japanese beetles
- Tomato hornworms
- Cutworms
- Snails
- Flea beetles
- Caterpillars
- Thrips
- Mealybugs
- Vine weevil
- Leaf miners
- Codling moth

Out of all of these, aphids and slugs are the most common pests you'll come across. Squash vine borers and bugs attack any squash plant; however, these can be taken care of by planting resistant varieties. Japanese beetles' copper-colored wings and metallic heads are easy to spot. The same goes for tomato hornworms and cutworms, which are moth larvae, resembling tiny caterpillars. Small infestations can be dealt with by physically removing the pests, but you'll need more effective control methods to take care of them in larger numbers.

It's tempting to bring out the big guns and drench your plants in chemical insecticides. However, it's important to remember that your garden is an ecosystem driven by diversity. A delicate balance exists between your garden and the life it supports, including a range of beneficial insects and microorganisms. The chemicals used in commercially available pesticides often disrupt this balance. In contrast, natural controls are not only effective against a large number of pests but economical as well.

The elevated design of raised beds limits pest invasions; however, it can't eliminate them entirely. Here are some tips to prevent predatory species from taking over your garden and wreaking havoc on your crops:

1. **Monitor For Signs of Pest Infestations** - The presence of holes in the leaves, patches of discoloration, limp stems, yellowing leaves, and egg clusters all signal trouble. Inspecting the leaves and stems of your plants regularly can help catch the culprits early on, preventing serious damage. Make sure to deadhead and prune diseased plant parts and destroy plant debris to curb the spread of disease.

2. **Try Mulching** - Mulching not only helps the soil retain moisture and suppress weeds, it can possibly repel various pests. For example, cedar and cypress bark when used as mulch ward off a number of nibbling insects. However, keep in mind that some woods do the opposite, attracting bugs like roaches, termites, carpenter ants, and earwigs.

3. **Employ natural predators** - Put an end to harmful pests by inviting their natural predators. Lady beetles, lacewings, predatory wasps, and praying mantis will take care of most pests. Throw them a feast of dill, cilantro, calendula, marigolds, alyssums, and yarrow and they'll come marching to your garden.

4. **Consistent Watering** - Your plant stands a better chance of fighting off pests and diseases when it's not battling with heat and water stress. Proper watering increases your plant's ability to defend itself and is the best prevention strategy against diseases of all kinds.

5. **Try companion planting** - Pair your crops with pest-deterring plants such as yarrow, mint, coriander, fennel, basil, catnip, yarrow, dill, and lemongrass and you're good to go!

Methods of Control

There are various methods of control you can use to keep pest populations in check. Let's explore some solutions to put an end to pests invading your beloved garden.

Diatomaceous Earth

This eco-friendly, non-toxic powder is made from the fossilized remains of diatoms, a group of tiny aquatic organisms called plankton. Their exoskeleton is made up of silica. When crushed into a fine powder, it can be potentially fatal for a number of pests. The powder has a rather coarse texture and damages the exoskeleton of insects on contact. A thin, even layer of the powder, sprinkled around the bed is enough to restrict entry. The only downside to DE is that it'll get washed away by heavy rains, requiring reapplication.

Physical Barriers

Physically stopping the pests from entering the raised bed or your garden is an effective way to protect your plants. Collars, fabric, mesh, and fencing are some common barrier materials that you can use. Sticky traps are also an excellent option. They can also help you identify the particular pests in your area for targeted treatment. Simply place them around each bed to capture adult insects, preventing them from laying their parasitic larvae.

Plant covers help protect plants from extreme weather conditions while warding off pests. They can hinder pollination; however, you can avoid this by removing the covers when the plants start flowering. Hand pollination is another option you can explore.

Floating row covers are particularly effective for stubborn pests impervious to other treatments. They consist of a thin white fabric, made from spun polyester, that can be placed on the soil or fixed to a frame and placed on the plants. If you use the fabric on its own, you'll need to stake it using landscape staples or weights to stop it from blowing away in the wind. Fasten the fabric around the bed; however, make sure to leave it slack enough to allow the plant to grow. For taller plants, you'll have to build row cover frames from PEX pipes or wood. Floating row covers are easy to use on raised beds.

Intercropping

Growing several plants together in the raised beds can help repel pests. Grouping the same plant next to each other makes them an easy target. Toss a few pest-repellent species in the mix and you've added another layer of protection.

Nematodes

These microscopic organisms are a lifesaver for pest-infested gardens; they're effective against more than 200 species of insects. These include the sneaky, but deadly cutworms, cabbage maggots, raspberry crown borers, root weevil larvae, and most beetles. They're easily available in the market, a single packet containing up to a million nematodes.

The application is quite simple. You just need to mix them with water and apply to the soil. They get to work in moist soil, preying on pests. They're harmless to humans and pets, sparing a huge variety of beneficial insects like earthworms and pollinators. By applying them to raised beds, you can target the larval stage of specific soil-dwelling parasites known for causing most of the damage to plants. Just make sure to read the instructions on the packet and buy the right kind, since different nematodes target different insect populations.

Home Remedies

You don't always have to buy expensive chemical pesticides to take out the tiny bugs wreaking havoc on your garden. In addition to being heavy on the pocket, chemical pesticides tend to kill a broad spectrum of insects indiscriminately. So you get rid of the harmful pests ruining your garden along with a handful of beneficial insects that could've helped you out in the long run.

Why spend all that money on a temporary solution when some of the most powerful pest deterrents are out there sitting in your kitchen cabinet? Garlic, chili pepper powder, baking soda, neem oil, dish soap, and vegetable oil. Diluted concentrations of these can be used to repel soft-bodied insects such as aphids, mealybugs, lace bugs, leafhoppers, and thrips. Simply mix one part of your ingredient of choice with two or three parts water in a spray bottle and spritz away!

Neem oil is a product extracted from neem trees grown in India, and it's the seeds of these trees that contain salannin, an insect repellent. Diluted neem oil when sprayed on the foliage, destroys adult insects as well as their eggs and larvae. It's effective against a large number of pests including beetles, spider mites, aphids, whiteflies, and leaf-eating caterpillars. Apply until the plant is thoroughly wet, ensuring the affected leaves are coated. Remember to reapply after heavy rains.

Copper Mesh

The slime trails weaving around your tomato seedlings are a sign of snails or slugs. These tiny creatures aren't always bad news. Many species of slugs and snails help break down organic matter, enriching the soil with nutrients. They're considered a valuable part of the garden ecosystem. However, some species feed on young green growth and must be dealt with.

Copper mesh tape placed around the bed's perimeter keeps the slugs and snails out. The copper oxidizes and produces numerous toxic salts, sending them crawling in the opposite direction. Avoid placing the tape too close to the ground or it could get covered in dirt and lose its efficacy. You can also use diatomaceous earth to keep the hungry slugs away from a particular raised bed. Handpick the trespassers inside the bed and line the edges of the bed with the powder to prevent future visits.

Ferric Phosphate

Ferric phosphate is another soil treatment you can try. It causes the slugs and snails to shrivel up and die; however, it's non-toxic to other insects and wildlife. Just stay away from the chelated form of ferric phosphate, which is toxic to dogs and other animals. Remember to read the labels and avoid using more than the needed amount. A few pellets scattered around the bed are all you need to do the trick.

Keeping Wildlife Out of Your Raised Beds

An advantage of growing plants in raised beds is that you don't have to shun all kinds of animals from your garden. Hedgehogs, birds, and other small animals play important roles in the garden ecosystems, often causing home growers to take their presence into account while designing their gardens. While the small animals breathe life into your home garden, you'll want to limit their access to your raised beds to prevent crop damage.

Raised beds that are 36 inches tall are usually sufficient to keep out some animals like rabbits. You can also attach a hardware cloth to the bottom of the bed, extending it up the insides a few inches to prevent rodents from burrowing into the bed from underneath. A garden cloche or floating row cover attached to the bed frame offers further protection. You can also use metal rebars to create a frame for the cover. Fix the bars along the length of the bed with 24-inch spaces in between, with the top rebar forming a U shape. Attach fabric or plastic to this frame for protection. This will also prevent birds from pecking on your harvest. However, make sure that the fabric is pulled tight so the birds don't get tangled in the netting.

Since birds play an important role in the garden ecosystem, you want to take a proactive approach to minimize damage to your plants without causing them harm or driving them away entirely. Planting native fruiting bushes away from your crops is one way to divert their attention from your harvest. Copses and hedgerows further help preserve bird habitat, encouraging them to work the garden soil and eliminate pests.

DIY Pest Cover

This is a useful add-on for raised beds to keep pests and small animals from nibbling on your plants. It's basically a lid that fits the top and inside of the raised bed. Let's look at the supplies you'll need to build one:

Supplies

- Plywood strips (1″ x 2″ x 8′)
- Wood screws (Box of #8, 1 and a half inch)
- White screen fabric
- Thread
- Screen door handles (optional)

Tools Required

- Screwdriver
- Electric drill
- Staple gun
- Measuring tape
- Scissors or knife

Instructions

1. Measure the inside width and length of your raised beds before heading to the home center for the plywood strips. Don't measure right to the edge. Make sure to leave some wiggle room as compensation for the thickness of the wood pieces.

2. Decide how tall you want the cover then multiply the number by four for the four corners. The total of these measurements will determine how many strips of wood you need. For example, for raised beds that are 5 feet square, you'll need eight 8-foot strips. Four for the top and four for the bottom. For each 8-foot piece, cut a 3-foot piece of leftover. You'll need to use four 3-foot leftover pieces for the sides of the cover's 2 feet tall.

3. Cut the eight pieces for the top and bottom, drill pilot holes for the screws, and fasten the four pieces together.

4. Check the measurements by placing the frame on the raised bed. Now is the time to make any adjustments, if required.

5. Repeat step 2 of the remaining four pieces.

6. Join the four side pieces to one of the frames with screws.

7. Flip the frame with the side pieces over and line it up with the other frame below. Join the side pieces to that one and your pest cover is almost ready.

8. Use staples to attach the fabric to the top frame.

9. Cover the sides, making sure to pull the fabric tightly over the frame before stapling it in place.

10. Use threads to sew any pieces of the fabric together if they seem to be overlapping.

11. Attach two screen door handles to the top so you can easily lift the frame, and your pest cover will be ready for use.

Figure 13: Example of a physical protection over a raised bed.

Turning your garden into a safe haven for friendly animals will not only create a pleasant environment, but also help your plants in the long run. Birds flocking to your garden can take care of insects, slugs, snails, and a number of other pests that may cause harm to your crops. Here are some tips to draw hedgehogs, birds, pollinating insects, and other small animals to your garden:

1. **Select the right plants** - Opt for vibrant and fragrant plants like lavender, rosemary, medicinal sage, garden thyme, and peonies to bring butterflies, bees, and other pollinators swarming to your garden.

2. **Build an insect hotel** - Pollinating insects are crucial if you want your plants to bear fruit. Insect hotels provide the tiny winged helpers food and shelter to lay their eggs. It's a small frame filled with twigs, stems, vines, and sticks. You can either build a small box or use a can or some other hollow object and place them around your garden in sheltered, sunny spots.

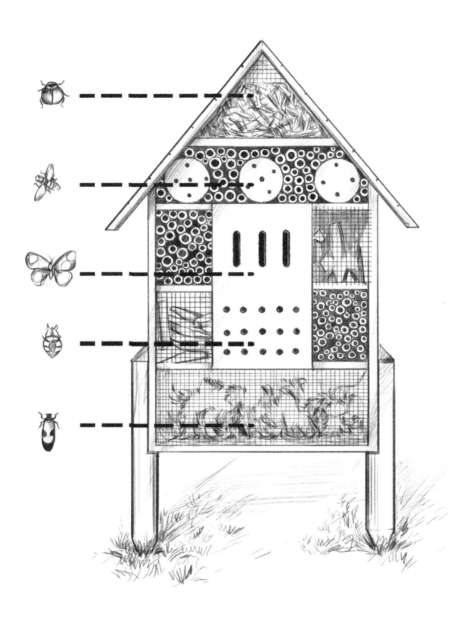

Figure 14: DIY insect hotel.

3.   Include bird feeders - Something as simple as putting out a bowl or pot of water can help attract more birds to your garden. If your budget allows, install a bird bath in your garden and hang a few bird feeders. These helpful creatures dig out the pests hidden deep in your soil, taking care of the slugs and snails that may harm your young plants.

4. **Install a few bird boxes** - I have a beautiful pair of swallows living in the bird box in my garden that greet me with their cheerful chirps whenever I visit. Bird boxes provide a safe place for birds to breed and make your garden their home. Be sure to check the boxes from time to time to make sure they're safe for your tiny friends. Hedges made of ivy, goat's bough, lilac, yew, and hazel may also attract birds for nesting.

Figure 15: Bird boxes invite songbirds.

5.   Opt for natural methods of control - I always recommend going for non-toxic and organic pesticides to protect beneficial insects and animals. Lizards are often misunderstood and identified as the enemy when they're anything but. They prey on smaller insects and their parasitic larvae, making them a welcome addition to home gardens. Mulch your garden regularly to attract more of these tiny helpers to take care of the pests. Create small spaces for them with a brick or concrete block and avoid using chemical pesticides.

6.   Bring in the hedgehogs - Same as birds and other pollinators, hedgehogs are beneficial to the garden ecosystem as these nocturnal animals prey on many pests. Create small sheltered places for them to hide in during the day where they can hibernate in peace. Be careful not to disturb them during the day, especially during fall. These adorable little helpers will also appreciate it if you leave out a bit of water for them in a small bowl, so they can have a drink while they work tirelessly at night to rid your garden of pests.

Figure 16: Hedgehog and lizard hotels.

Key Takeaways

This marks the end of our journey! We learned about the various pests we may come across in our garden and how to limit and eliminate them so our plants can thrive. We looked at different control methods and how we can protect our plants without harming useful insects and animals. Our garden is an ecosystem and home to many small animals and we should do the best we can to keep it as such. Moreover, we should try out ways to draw beneficial critters to our garden to make our plants flourish!

Conclusion

When I started raising-bed gardening, I had no clue I'd grow to love it as much as I do now. I started with a single raised bed then gradually expanded my set up to include four. I remember my neighbor helping me with the wheelbarrow to fill it with soil. Soon my backyard was teeming with potatoes, leeks, garlic, peas, beans, tomatoes, and celery. What amazed me the most was how little weeding the beds required! I spent most of my childhood gardening and pulling those weeds out of the soil had always been my least favorite task.

This was ten years ago. Now, all my food comes from my own backyard and grocery trips are few and far between. The first few raised beds I clumsily assembled all those years ago have gotten an upgrade and there have been many new—and much better looking—additions. I grow almost everything from seeds in the deep winter inside my house under grow lights.

What started as a fun experiment, transformed me into a full-time gardener, cutting my grocery bills in half! My kids devour the home grown fruits and vegetables during mealtimes and I can't help but feel proud of what I managed to accomplish. Growing up on my grandparents' farm, I knew the joy of biting into sun-ripened tomatoes and juicy red apples, warm to the touch, and wanted my kids to experience it. I wrote this book because I want other people to experience the same feeling.

We started this book by learning about the many benefits these garden beds have to offer and their different types. Over the next few chapters, we looked at the importance of understanding our space and planning accordingly, the dimensions of raised bed frames, garden layouts, and ways to maximize our space.

We explored the various materials we can use for constructing raised beds and went over step-by-step instructions to build them. We discussed the relationship between good soil health and plant growth and the steps we can take to improve and maintain it. Midway through the book, we looked at the crops best suited for growth in raised beds and the different planting methods we can choose from. We learned about the significance of getting spacing right and the advantages of companion planting.

The chapter on planting guides provided us with a glimpse of what raised-bed gardening looks like over the space of a year. We looked at some of the tasks that would keep us occupied, the best time to get them done, and the plants we should grow. Finally, we moved on to irrigation methods and harvesting techniques before delving into the best ways to achieve pest control.

I'm going to end this book by encouraging you to find your green thumb and take the first step toward transforming your garden. While raised beds undoubtedly make gardening a lot easier, it's the gardeners' resolve that matters the most. Don't be discouraged by failure and keep trying to find what works best for your plants. Remember, you're in charge of the small piece of land you occupy on this planet. Whether it lays barren or bursts forth with luscious fruits and vegetables is up to you!

Thanks for Reading, Please Leave a Review!

I would be *incredibly appreciative* if you could rate my book or leave a review on **Amazon**.

Just scan this QR code with your phone, or visit the https://Rbpaperback.SophieMckay.com link to land directly on the book's Amazon review page.

Your review not only helps me create better books, but also helps more fellow gardener experience success in the garden and put healthy food on their family's table.

Thank you!

Grab your FREE gifts!

Sophie McKay's Seed Starting & Planting Calculator + The Ultimate Guide to Organic Weed Management

In these free resources, you will discover:

- The perfect Seed Starting and Planting times for YOUR region or zone
- The 8 Organic Weed Removal Methods
- The 6 best and proven Weed Management Methods
- The tools you did NOT know you need for a weed-free garden
- How weeds can help your yard
- How to identify which weed is good and which is bad for a yard or garden
- The difference between Invasive and Noxious Weeds

Get your FREE copy today by visiting:
https://sophiemckay.com/free-resources/

Unlock the Secrets to Thriving Fruit Tree Gardens!

Transform your backyard orchard dreams into reality with 'Beginner's Guide to Growing Fruit Trees Fast and Easy.' Your guide on this road will be Sophie McKay, an avid gardener and an emerging author in gardening, permaculture, and sustainability. She'll share her best tips and tricks to ensure your gardening journey succeeds.

From **efficient** garden **layout design to selecting healthy trees, introducing pruning and grafting basics, mastering sustainable pest management, and creating a permaculture-inspired food forest**—this guide is your go-to resource for cultivating a vibrant and fruitful orchard. With practical insights, rejuvenating techniques, and seasonal care tips, embark on a sustainable gardening success story.

Just **scan this QR code** with your phone, or visit the https://BuyFTG.SophieMckay.com link to land directly book's Amazon page.

If You Liked This Book, Try This One Too!

Sophie's fantastic new book, **The Beginner's Guide to Successful Container Gardening**, is now published!

Inside, **you will learn about the basics of container gardening**, including **selecting the right container, soil, and plants** for all your needs. You will also learn about the specific requirements of different types of plants, and how to care for them throughout the growing season. **Whether you're a seasoned gardener or just getting started, this book has something for everyone.**

So if you're ready for some more inspiration, check out this book now to keep your garden thriving all year round with **25+ proven DIY methods for composting, companion planting, seed saving, water management and pest control!**

So what are you waiting for? Grab it for yourself!

Just **scan this QR code** with your phone, or visit the https://Container.SophieMckay.com link to land directly on the book's Amazon page.

Welcome to Permaculture!

Unlock the secrets of a resilient garden! Discover permaculture design and **learn how to grow your own food in harmony with nature**.

Join Sophie on a guided tour and create your own **sustainable permaculture garden** with confidence. Success guaranteed!

Just scan this QR code with your phone, or visit the https://book.SophieMckay.com link to land directly on the book's Amazon page.

Bibliography

Bordessa, K. (2021, July 16). *Container Vegetable Gardening for Beginners*. Attainable Sustainable.

Can You Start Composting in Urban Areas? (2019, June 24). Greenhouse Emporium.

Chadwick, P. (2020, October 5). *Guidelines for Harvesting Vegetables*. Piedmont Master Gardeners.

Chase, A. (n.d.). *10 Ways to Keep Your Garden Healthy - FineGardening*. Fine Gardening. Retrieved September 12, 2022.

Caufield, C. (2023, November 8). *How to build a herb spiral — Backyard Harvest Project*. Backyard Harvest Project. Retrieved April 25, 2024, from https://www.backyardharvestproject.com/blog/garden-project-herb-spiral-part-1

DeJohn, S. (2023, September 14). *Best Materials for Raised Beds*. Gardener's Supply. Retrieved April 21, 2024, from https://www.gardeners.com/how-to/materials-for-raised-beds/9578.html

DeVore, S. (2019). *Transplant vs Direct Sow: Which Method to Use*. Harris Seeds. Retrieved June 24, 2024, from https://www.harrisseeds.com/blogs/homegrown/transplant-vs-direct-sow

Engels, J. (2016, November 18). *How and Why to Rotate Your Annual Crops - The Permaculture Research Institute*. Permaculture Research Institute.

Fischer, N. (2018, January 4). *The 14 Best Seed Companies to Plant in Your Organic Garden*. Nature's Path.

Harvesting Guide. (n.d.). Kellogg Garden Products.

Holdsworth, G. (2021). *Raised Bed Pest Cover - FineGardening*. Fine Gardening. Retrieved July 13, 2024, from https://www.finegardening.com/article/raised-bed-pest-cover

How To Plan for Companion Planting in Raised Beds — Platt Hill Nursery, Chicago. (2023, February 27). Platt Hill Nursery. Retrieved June 24, 2024, from https://platthillnursery.com/mapping-your-raised-garden-beds-chicago/

Judd, A. S. (n.d.). *Best Way to Water Raised-Bed Gardens*. Growing In The Garden.

McKay, S. (2022). *The Practical Permaculture Project*.

McKay, S. (2023). *Beginners Guide to Successful Container Gardening*.

Masabni, J. (n.d.). *Mulching - Should you water before or after mulching?* Texas A&M AgriLife Extension.

Mayntz, M. (2021, March 15). *Different Types of Hummingbird Feeders*. The Spruce.

Patterson, S. (n.d.). *Which Soil Is Best for Plant Growth? | LoveToKnow*. Garden.

Porter, B. (2020, April 16). *Plant Spacing in Raised Beds*. The Seasonal Homestead. Retrieved June 24, 2024, from https://www.theseasonalhomestead.com/plant-spacing-in-raised-beds/

Proctors. (2022). *Planting Calendar For Fruits*. Proctors NPK. Retrieved July 14, 2024, from https://www.proctorsnpk.com/t/PlantingCalendarFruit

RHS. (2021). *Fruit gardening calendar*. RHS Campaign for School Gardening. Retrieved July 14, 2024, from https://schoolgardening.rhs.org.uk/Resources/Info-Sheet/Fruit-Gardening-Calendar

Romans, M. (2023, March 31). *Where to Place Your Garden: 4 Key Considerations*. Greater Lansing Food Bank. Retrieved April 15,

2024, from https://greaterlansingfoodbank.org/where-to-place-your-garden-4-key-considerations

SanSone, A. (2021, March 25). *15 Best Plants That Attract Pollinators - Best Flowers for Pollinators*. The Pioneer Woman.

Selection of Seeds- Factors To Consider While Selecting Seeds. (2016, May 7). Ugaoo.

Scott, A. (2019). *Raised Bed Garden Plan*. Must Love Lists. Retrieved July 3, 2024, from https://mustlovelists.com/raised-bed-garden-plan/

Sparks, M. (2023, April 21). *Month-by-Month Guide to Vegetable Gardening*. Real Simple. Retrieved July 3, 2024, from https://www.realsimple.com/home-organizing/gardening/outdoor/month-by-month-vegetable-gardening-guide

Urban Farmer. (2022). *Herb Growing Guide*. Urban Farmer. Retrieved July 14, 2024, from https://www.ufseeds.com/herb-growing-guide.html

Vinje, E. (2012, December 7). *How to Make Your Own Potting Soil*. Planet Natural.

Whittingham, J. (2012). *Fruit and Vegetables in Pots*. DK Pub.

Made in the USA
Coppell, TX
24 May 2025

49848478R00075